S0-ASN-945

Themes, Theories, and Therapy:

The Teaching of Writing in College

THE CARNEGIE SERIES IN AMERICAN EDUCATION

The books in this series have resulted from studies made under grants from the Carnegie Corporation of New York and from time to time studies supported by The Carnegie Foundation for the Advancement of Teaching. These books are published by McGraw-Hill in recognition of their importance to the future of American education.

The Corporation, a philanthropic foundation established in 1911 by Andrew Carnegie for the advancement and diffusion of knowledge and understanding, has a continuing interest in the improvement of American education. It financed the studies in this series to provide facts and recommendations which would be useful to all those who make or influence the decisions which shape American educational policies and institutions.

The statements made and views expressed in these books are solely the responsibility of the authors.

Books Published

Berelson · Graduate Education in the United States
Clark · The Open Door College: A Case Study
Cleveland · The Overseas American
Conant · The American High School Today
Corson · Governance of Colleges and Universities
Dodds · The Academic President—Educator or Caretaker?
Glenny · Autonomy of Public Colleges
Henninger · The Technical Institute in America
Kitzhaber · Themes, Theories, and Therapy: The Teaching of Writing in College
McConnell · A General Pattern for American Public Higher Education
Medsker · The Junior College: Progress and Prospect
Perkins and Snell · The Education of Historians in the United States
Pierson · The Education of American Businessmen
Thomas · The Search for a Common Learning: General Education, 1800–1960
Weidner · The World Role of Universities

808
K65

77529

PE
1068
US
KS
1963

Themes, Theories, and Therapy:

The Teaching of Writing in College

THE REPORT OF THE DARTMOUTH STUDY OF STUDENT WRITING

Albert R. Kitzhaber

University of Oregon

McGraw-Hill Book Company, Inc.

New York   San Francisco   Toronto   London

GOSHEN COLLEGE LIBRARY
GOSHEN, INDIANA

THEMES, THEORIES, AND THERAPY: The Teaching
of Writing in College

Copyright © 1963 by the McGraw-Hill Book Company, Inc. All Rights
Reserved. Printed in the United States of America. This book, or parts
thereof, may not be reproduced in any form without permission of
the publishers. *Library of Congress Catalog Card Number* 63–13142

To the memory of
Porter G. Perrin

Acknowledgments

I want to express my sincere thanks to the members of the English department at Dartmouth College who supplied me with papers by their students and to other members of the Dartmouth faculty for papers by sophomores, juniors, and seniors; to Mrs. Phyllis Warfel, who helped greatly with the analysis of student writing; to Prof. Clark Horton of Dartmouth, whose expert help with the statistical aspect of the error study was indispensable; and to Dean Arthur E. Jensen of Dartmouth, whose advice and support throughout the study were equally invaluable.

I am indebted also to the many English department chairmen and directors of freshman English who sent me information about the writing programs at their institutions and particularly to those who gave me so much of their time when I visited their campuses to discuss their courses with them.

To Vincent E. Gillespie, now of the University of Kansas, I owe a heavy debt of gratitude for the preparatory work that he did for the study in 1959–1960 and for help during the following year, when we worked together at Dartmouth.

A number of people were kind enough to read part or all of the manuscript and give me their reactions, from all of which I have tried to profit. These include in particular three of my former colleagues in the English department at Dartmouth, Profs. William Crawford, Henry Terrie, and Frank Brady. Prof. Edward Green of the psychology department at Dartmouth and Dr. Devra Rowland, formerly of Fairleigh Dickinson University, read the pages dealing with teaching machines; Profs. Harold Allen of the University of Minnesota and Wayne O'Neil of the University of Oregon read those on linguistics. Dr. Rowland's suggestions were especially detailed and helpful. The entire manuscript was read by Profs. Wallace W. Douglas and Walter Rideout of Northwestern University, Richard M. Ludwig of Princeton University, James B. Meriwether of the University of North Carolina, and Robert M. Gorrell of the University of Nevada. I thank all of these for their generous help and must make it clear that whatever errors or defects remain in the book are entirely my fault, not theirs.

Finally, I am grateful to Mr. Frederick H. Jackson and Miss Margaret E. Mahoney of the Carnegie Corporation of New York for their advice, and to the Corporation itself for the grant that made the study possible. Mr. Thomas R. Carskadon of the Twentieth Century Fund was most helpful in bringing the manuscript to publication.

Much of the first section of the report and part of the third appeared originally in *College English* and *English Journal*. This material is copyrighted by the National Council of Teachers of English and has been revised and used here with the permission of the Council.

Albert R. Kitzhaber

Introduction

In the autumn of 1958, Dartmouth College submitted a proposal to the Carnegie Corporation of New York requesting support for a study of the writing of college students. Behind this request lay two years of inquiry and discussion by an *ad hoc* committee of the faculty. The committee recognized that although Dartmouth is favored in the caliber of its students as the vast majority of colleges in the nation are not, a great many of the young men admitted are unable, at the time they enroll, to express their thoughts in writing that is clear, effective, and reasonably correct. Whether the blame for this inability rests principally on the lower schools, on home environment, or on other influences, it was clear that these circumstances lie outside the college's immediate control and that substantial improvement in them will be long on the way and difficult to bring about. For at least some years to come, Dartmouth will continue to get students of superior intelligence who are handicapped by the inability to write with correctness and precision and who will need training in the principles and practice of written discourse if they are to become liberally educated men.

For this reason the college requires nearly all entering students to take further instruction in composition in the freshman English courses. The committee was persuaded that at the end of these courses most students write better than they do at the beginning, as indeed they should; but the degree of improvement does not always seem to be in proportion to the magnitude of the effort. The first question, therefore, that the committee hoped the study would answer was: Can English composition at Dartmouth be taught more effectively in the required freshman English courses than it is now?

There was a second question, equally important. Regardless of how much the writing skill of Dartmouth students improves in freshman English, the committee had the impression that the improvement frequently does not last. Once freshman English is completed, many students appear to fall back into their old habits and write as carelessly as they did before. The committee was conscious that the faculty at large often regards good student writing as the particular responsibility of the English department; freshman English, many people think, ought to fix, once and for all, the habits of correct usage and clear and orderly writing so that teachers in other departments need take no special pains about these matters. If the course cannot establish these habits, they argue, why is it required?

The committee believed that such a view is mistaken, that the English department can set a standard for good writing in freshman English but that if students are to continue to write competently as sophomores, juniors, and seniors, the entire faculty must cooperate in helping to maintain the standard of quality set in the freshman year. A second question, then, was: Can anything be done to ensure that students will continue to write at least as well after they have left freshman English as they do while they are taking it? Or, to put the question another way: What is the responsibility of the general faculty toward maintaining acceptable standards of writing among their students, and can the faculty be persuaded to accept that responsibility more fully?

The committee hoped that the study would produce plans for a more effective freshman composition program and recommend measures and devices that would help to bring about and sustain a college-wide effort to keep students writing well in all courses. And, because the committee was aware that dissatisfaction with the writing of college students is well-nigh universal, there was some hope that the results of a close study of the problem of teaching writing at one college would have considerable interest for other colleges as well.

The proposal was favorably received by officials of the Carnegie Corporation, and a grant was accordingly made to Dartmouth in support of the project.

Contents

Chapter 1

Teaching English Composition in College

PROBLEMS

Every fall thousands upon thousands of American young people enter college. Some of them come with no clear notion of what they want to study or what career they want to prepare for and are impelled only by a vague desire to "get a college education." Others know, or think they know, exactly what they want—degrees in engineering, chemistry, nuclear physics, law, home economics, business administration, journalism. Many girls frankly want only a college-educated husband because of his greater earning power, and they plan to remain students just long enough to get one, then quit to go to work or have babies. But no matter what the plans of the young people may be, no matter what their interests or expectations, they know they must count on one inevitable curricular fact: They will have to take freshman English. They will have been prepared for this course in various ways by their high school teachers—warned, threatened, cajoled, sometimes taught—but few of them look forward to it with confidence, fewer still with pleasure. Freshman English is one of those things like spinach and tetanus shots that young people put up with because their elders say they must. Whether it is called "Freshman English," "English Composition," "Freshman Rhetoric," or "Communication Skills," this course has been a staple of freshman studies for three-quarters of a century and is by far the most populous in the American college curriculum.

Only a few English departments, nearly always at small colleges with highly selective admission policies, have declined to accept responsibility for the course. "It is our assumption," says the chairman at one such college, "that students entering college should have acquired this skill [writing] in secondary school and that application and development of such skill is best handled in terms of the disciplines in which they actually have to do their writing." Other English departments, also most commonly in selective colleges, have converted the usual course in freshman composition into one in literature. "As far back as 1940," writes another chairman, "we abandoned an old-fashioned English A composition course on the ground that it bored the better students and didn't really help anyone very much. We substituted a freshman course in literature, a course in critical analysis with a good deal of writing in it. . . ."

But these departments, at least so far, are exceptions. In spite of Prof. Warner Rice's call for the abolition of freshman composition,[1] it is still very much with us, and the great majority of college English departments, though they often grumble about the course, still offer it and not infrequently defend it.

The course is supported by two distinct arguments, sometimes advanced separately, more often combined in varying proportions. The first of these is practical: The course exists to provide immediate therapy for students whose academic future is clouded by their inability to manage the written form of English with reasonable ease, precision, and correctness. According to this argument the course must remedy deficiencies of high school training in English and develop each student's writing skill to the level of competence required by college work. This is the "service" concept of the course. It assumes that the student should benefit in an immediate and practical way from the training offered in the course: he should henceforth write with due regard for the amenities of English prose, whether he is taking a sophomore course in history or a senior course in economics. The student's other teachers should likewise enjoy a practical benefit, for they should be able to assume that the student has been taught to write with ease, precision, and correctness in the freshman English course; and therefore they are under no obligation to police the student's writing in their own courses. If the student does not write well, the fault lies with the English department, and one discharges one's responsibility in the

---

[1] "A Proposal for the Abolition of Freshman English, as It Is Now Commonly Taught, from the College Curriculum," *College English*, 21:361–367, 1960.

matter by saying so in faculty meetings. The origin of the service notion, which can be traced back seventy-five or a hundred years, need not be gone into here; it is enough to say that it rose from powerful social and educational pressures in the latter half of the nineteenth century and was encouraged by the increasing compartmentalization of the college curriculum in those years and by the confusion of functions that attended the disappearance of departments of rhetoric and oratory and the rise of departments of English. Since required freshman English first appeared at Harvard in 1885, the prevailing view has been that this is a service course.[2]

The other argument supporting freshman English is not practical but liberal. This argument assumes that the primary purpose of the course is to focus the student's attention on fundamental principles of clear thinking and the clear and effective written expression of that thinking and to give him disciplined practice in applying the principles. This kind of intellectual training, it is argued, is essential in any system of liberal education and is rigorous enough to merit inclusion without apology in a college or university curriculum; it is something that should have been begun in the lower schools but could not by any means have been disposed of there. In so far as control of the content of any subject requires a student to be able to organize and present this content in written language, the argument goes, instruction in all courses should aim at this kind of discipline. The difference in this regard between other courses and the freshman English course is that in the latter the principles of clear thinking and effective expression—the principles of logic and rhetoric—and their successful application are at the center of attention, the primary concern of the course. The work of other courses should foster the same discipline but direct it toward

[2] A required course in "Sophomore Rhetoric" had been offered at Harvard for some years before this under the direction of Adams Sherman Hill, who became Boylston Professor of Rhetoric and Oratory in 1876. In 1879 Hill urged that the course be moved to the freshman year, but the change does not appear to have been made until 1885. The new course, called "English A," was widely imitated by other colleges. [See Adams Sherman Hill, "An Answer to the Cry for More English," reprinted in *Twenty Years of School and College English*, Cambridge, Mass.: Harvard University Press, 1896, p. 12; and C. H. Grandgent, "The Modern Languages," in S. E. Morison, ed., *The Development of Harvard University Since the Inauguration of President Eliot, 1869–1929*, Cambridge, Mass.: Harvard University Press, 1930, p. 75.]

the varying demands of the specific subject matters with which the courses deal.

In part because of these varying views of the essential purpose of the course, freshman English has assumed an enormous variety of forms from one campus to another. But there are other reasons, too, for its diversity. One is that the course in many colleges and universities is staffed primarily by graduate students and junior instructors who, though they are expected to carry out departmental policy toward the course in their classrooms, have little or no voice in determining this policy. The content and structure, for better or worse, are likely to be determined by the preferences of the director of the course or the department chairman, who usually does not teach the course (or if he does, teaches special sections of bright students). Being somewhat insulated from the way their policies work out in most classrooms, the administrators are more free to indulge their particular professional interests or apply their pet theories. Thus one seldom finds a course stressing semantics or linguistics without also finding a disciple of Bloomfield or Korzybski somewhere in a position of influence.

Another reason for the bewildering diversity of freshman English courses is that in a period of ten or fifteen weeks some improvement in writing usually takes place no matter what is in the course, as long as the students are reasonably normal and are doing some writing under supervision. The improvement may be, as one director of freshman English has said, no more than a temporarily conditioned reflex, visible only in such changes as a growing preference for *similar* instead of *similiar* and for sentences that have both a subject and a verb. But the fact of improvement can be cited in defense of this or that course pattern or content.

Still another reason is that semantics, logic, rhetoric, linguistics, literature, literary criticism, all are, or easily can be, related more or less directly to the teaching of writing since all deal with language and the principles of its use. Though a substantial carryover from the study of one or more of these subjects to skill in writing has never been conclusively proved, such a transfer can at least be persuasively argued. Thus a course emphasizing literature is defended on the grounds that the principles of good writing are necessarily derived from the practice of good writers, and standard literature comprises this practice. Or a course based on logic is defended with the argument that habits of consecutive thought are indispensable to good expository writing, and it is the business of logic to foster such habits. Moreover, all of these subjects are worth teaching in themselves and can be justified on this basis as well as on that of their relevance to the teaching of writing.

Finally, and most important, it is nearly impossible—perhaps really impossible—to prove or disprove the effectiveness of a particular course pattern and say that *because* the course emphasizes great literature or semantics or rhetoric, *therefore* the students taking it learn to write with greater skill and fluency. If a student does indeed write better at the end of a course in composition than he did at the beginning, many explanations for the phenomenon are possible. It may be that the particular course content was responsible, or that the enforced practice in writing was responsible. Perhaps the change was due to the expertness of the teacher—or, if not to his expertness, to his enthusiasm, his rapport with the particular student who improved. The improvement may be the result simply of increased maturity in the student; a dozen or fifteen weeks are not a long time in a person's life, but in the first semester of college a student can sometimes mature remarkably, compressing into this little space changes that under less urgent circumstances might take several times as long. It may be that the improvement is due to the student's living, perhaps for the first time in his life, in an intellectual community, in an environment in which ideas are important and brains fashionable. Perhaps the student has a natural and heretofore dormant facility for language, and some one of the many influences to which he has been exposed in his first term at college has brought it to life. Possibly the improvement may be credited to the influence of a teacher of some other course who has made the student see for the first time the relation between precision of thought and precision of utterance, using the data of a subject that happens to mean a great deal to the student—physics, say, to a student interested in science.

But consider the opposite situation: Suppose that after a course in English composition the student does *not* write better than he did at the beginning. What then? His lack of improvement may be due to his own stupidity or laziness or carelessness. He may be one of those unfortunates who suffer from a low aptitude for language, though often he may have a compensating talent for mathematics.

Perhaps he has trouble because he grew up in a home where no one read books and where the language that he heard was not only a different dialect from the one he is expected to learn in college but was careless, imprecise, cliché-ridden. Perhaps he had poor schooling or moved too often from one school to another so that he never had consecutive instruction. It may be that his English teacher's efforts to instill habits of correctness and coherence and precision of statement have been nullified by counterinfluences in other courses where teachers tolerate sloppy writing and say that "it's only the ideas that count." The student's friends may exert the same kind of counterinfluence; so may newspapers, radio, television, magazines. The student may have failed to improve simply because he was not well taught in the freshman English course—through the teacher's ignorance, careless correction of papers, inept writing assignments, or through personal antagonism between teacher and student. Or finally, the student may write no better at the end of the course than at the beginning because the content of the course may have been inappropriate to the teaching of composition.

The trouble is that the student sees his English teacher for at best only three or four hours a week and is busy with the work of the course perhaps another four or five hours. But during all his waking hours he is talking or listening or reading or thinking silently, and in all of these activities he is using language and by this use strengthening some habits and weakening others. The influences to which he is subject as he moves about in this linguistic universe may reinforce the lessons of the English class—or undermine them. Whichever happens, the effects of the English course cannot be isolated from the effects of a myriad of other influences which lie entirely outside the English teacher's control. And so we never know exactly how much the course in English composition has helped a student to improve his ability to write.

A final complication is that progress (or lack of it) in composition skill must always be measured subjectively; only the teacher's judgment can determine whether the last theme is better or worse than the first one, how much better or worse, and in what ways. General agreement on quality is of course not beyond reach. But even with sound professional training in the teaching of composition—something that cannot be generally assumed—teachers inevitably differ to some extent in their judgment of any given piece of writing. A composition of any length derives its form and substance from the particular human consciousness that uttered it and is therefore, in a strict sense, unprecedented. More than this, one can evaluate a student composition (or a magazine article, a play, a book) only by making countless individual judgments, most of them perhaps unconsciously. Each of these judgments depends ultimately on one's total previous experience with English as well as on one's system of personal values. The essential uniqueness of every human being makes it inevitable that no two judgments of something as complex as the written expression of an individual human personality can be alike in every respect. Sometimes the differences will be negligible; sometimes they will not.

It is evident, then, from what has just been said about the complexity of the writing process and of the task of teaching writing that there can be no real short cut to writing skill. That is, there can be no quick and painless way to develop a well-stocked mind, a disciplined intelligence, and a discriminating taste in language and fluency in its use. None of these can be acquired without hard work over a period of years, and it is preposterous to claim or to expect that any single course in either school or college, no matter how well taught or how intensively studied, can assure them. They are to a considerable extent the result of increasing maturity and of the total educational process acting on an intelligent mind. They are of course not absolutes which one either has or does not have; but in their higher manifestations they lie forever beyond the reach of many people, even some of those who attend the most highly selective colleges.

All teachers of academic subjects can help students to fill their minds, to train and focus their intellectual powers, and to make their use of language more exact; but English teachers and English courses have the opportunity to be especially helpful in moving students toward the second and third of these goals. More than other teachers and courses, they concentrate directly on the *quality* of written expression as well as the thinking embodied in it, on the principles that lie behind it, and on disciplined practice in applying these principles in written composition. But no one should expect a particular device or method or kind of subject matter in the English course to transform what must always be a slow and difficult process into one that is quick, easy, and unfailingly successful. The habit of good writing, like the habit of ethical conduct, is of slow growth; it is an aspect of a person's general intellectual development and cannot be greatly hastened apart from that development. This is not to say that writing instruction cannot be improved but only that a genuine panacea for poor writing does not seem at all likely and that to hope for one is naïve.[3]

THE PRESENT STATE
OF FRESHMAN COMPOSITION

College English professors have always been generous of advice to their high school colleagues, telling them what they should be doing that they are not and what they are doing that they should not be. Lately, moved by the general concern for improving American secondary education in the missile age, they have been even freer with their suggestions and have made them more specific. Such criticism is all to the good, even though the suggestions may sometimes be a little naïve and their Olympian tone a little annoying. With so large a proportion of high school graduates now entering college, the high schools should know what kind of academic preparation the colleges recommend.

The deficiencies of high school English courses and textbooks and of the professional preparation of many high school teachers of English have now been made a matter of public concern, and rightly so if any large-scale improvement is to be brought about. But what about the college English courses that nearly half of all high school graduates will take as freshmen? How good are these courses? How well are they being taught? What is in them? What are their announced purposes? What forms do they take? Do they avoid the weaknesses and errors for which college English teachers have blamed English courses in the secondary schools?

As part of the Dartmouth study a large number of syllabuses for college freshman English courses were analyzed in an effort to shed some light on these questions. The syllabuses came from ninety-five 4-year colleges and universities, but represented a total of ninety-eight individual course descriptions, since three universities on the list had separate programs in composition and in "communication." Except for the absence of junior colleges, the list is a fairly repre-

[3] See "A Look at 'Panaceas,'" pp. 73–92.

sentative cross section of American institutions of higher education. It includes both public and private universities, state colleges, teachers colleges, coeducational liberal arts colleges, liberal arts colleges for men only and for women only, and a few technical institutes primarily devoted to teaching engineering. All in all, there are fifty-eight publicly supported institutions on the list (including two municipal universities) and thirty-seven privately supported ones. Seventy-nine use the semester system, sixteen the quarter or "term" system. (These patterns affect to some extent the content and organization of the freshman English course.) Twenty-two of the colleges and universities are located in the Southeast and South, twenty-two in the Northeast, twenty-nine in the Midwest, and twenty-two in the West.

Information gathered from such sources does, to be sure, have certain obvious limitations no matter how representative the colleges are. For one thing, it goes out of date rapidly. The syllabuses were all for the academic year 1960–1961; those for even the following year would have shown changes in textbooks, in emphases, in requirements, in administrative patterns as a result of the constant tinkering that this course normally undergoes. (Often, however, the pattern of change is circular, one program adopting what has been abandoned somewhere else, and vice versa.) Another limitation is that course syllabuses are not all equally detailed. Some are literally book length, others consist of three or four mimeographed pages. Finally, as any teacher knows, a syllabus represents someone's notion of the ideal. What actually goes on in the classroom usually has some relation to the syllabus but in varying degrees, depending on the closeness of supervision and on the predilections of the individual teacher—his special interests, his opinion of the syllabus or of the textbooks or simply of the person who runs the program.

Aware of these limitations, the director of the study made an effort in 1961–1962 to surmount them as far as possible by visiting eighteen selected institutions on the list and checking the reliability of the syllabuses. The information contained in the syllabuses when corrected and added to by that gathered during the visits has considerable value as a description, accurate in the main, of freshman English courses as they now exist in a wide variety of American colleges and universities.

Anyone reading this many syllabuses or visiting this many freshman English programs—or even a fraction of the number—would
almost certainly be struck by at least three main weaknesses of the
course as it is now constituted. First, he would be impressed by the
confusion exhibited in the course—a widespread uncertainty about
aims, a bewildering variety of content, a frequent lack of progression
within the course. Second, he would notice a variety of administrative adjustments and precautions that indicate little confidence in
the expertness of those who teach it. And finally, he would notice
that the textbooks for this course are for the most part less rigorous and less scholarly than those for other college freshman
courses.

Confusion in purpose, content, and organization; inexpert teaching; poor textbooks: these criticisms will have a strangely familiar
sound to the ears of high school teachers, for they are exactly the
same criticisms that college teachers—often directors of freshman
English—have been making of English teaching in the high schools.
This is not to suggest that the criticisms of English teaching in the
high schools are without substance—far from it. But it is important
to realize that imperfection is not confined to the secondary schools.

These three general criticisms should be considered first to provide a background for the more specific account of practices and
tendencies that follows.

Aims, Content, Organization. In the most general terms, the
principal aim of freshman English is usually said to be the improvement of the student's ability to read and write, the assumption being
that these two skills necessarily go hand in hand. A state university
in the Southwest, for example, says modestly that its course "aims
to give the freshman student the minimum skills he will need to
function without disgrace as a reader and writer of English." The
so-called "communication" course adds improvement in the skills
of speaking and listening to the goals. And if the particular college
does not have a separate literature requirement, the statement of
aims usually includes teaching the student "to read literature with
understanding and appreciation." The only constant in all varieties
of the course is some provision for supervised practice in writing,
but, ironically, most of the confusion in freshman English stems
from differing notions of how writing ought to be taught. The
most diverse content may be dumped into the course on the grounds

that it will help the student learn to write better. The extent of the confusion can be dramatically illustrated by quoting half a dozen statements from as many different course syllabuses:

1. The Department of English affirms that the work of this first semester should train the student in *accuracy* in English composition. To achieve this general objective, we should include (1) work in the fundamentals, not in the intricacies, of English grammar. . . . Some knowledge of basic grammar . . . is essential to the student who seriously desires to speak and write his native tongue correctly. We should include also (2) extensive drill on the "mechanics" of composition—for example, work on correct spelling and punctuation, on smooth and varied sentence structure, on clear and effective expression of the thought. We should include (3) training in writing of unified, coherent, and generally effective paragraphs, since the writing of a paragraph will involve all of the basic disciplines of English composition. Finally, as time permits, we should include (4) reading, since through the reading of good writing by others the student may develop his own writing skills.

2. The general aim is to improve the student's ability to read and write through requiring substantial work with a significant body of ideas. Materials presenting living issues of the American cultural and intellectual heritage have been chosen both because of their usefulness in a language program and because they are worth knowing for their own sake. It is expected that the student will improve his ability to read by studying documents important in our national life, and that he will improve his ability to write by expressing on paper his own ideas about these issues.

3. Our course tries to motivate the student by acquainting him with semantic theory concerning the nature and importance of communication. . . . An increased knowledge of a second area—linguistics—ought also to supply motivation. . . . But there is no reason why the course should be confined to language problems. The book of readings permits the inclusion of subjects in which the students may have a stronger immediate interest.

4. A question may arise about the suitability of fiction or poetry or drama in a course which presents what appears to be

a program in expository writing. We feel very strongly that the omission of imaginative literature would be a great mistake. Without it, both the teacher and the student would be robbed of the kind of richness which can make teaching an art instead of a craft.

5. We believe that composition is best taught when it occupies the place of chief emphasis in a course and is not combined with a formal study of literature. . . . Our experience has led us to believe that our students are unprepared in writing largely because their high school or preparatory school teachers stressed literature rather than composition; that the study of literature, if introduced into a composition course, tends to push into the background the more needful work; that there is not time in a single semester to do justice both to a study of literature and to a study of composition; and that the study of literature is properly preceded by a study of language.

6. We still ask our students to write, and to write a good deal. But they are asked to write about the subject matter of the course, quite as they are in other courses in the college. And when we consider that our students are asked to learn about the phonemic structure of the spoken tongue, the relations of that structure to the spelling of the language in writing, the basic grammatical devices of spoken and written English, the logical conventions of classification, definition, induction, and deduction that inform an accurate use of the language in intelligent discourse, we find a great deal to write about, indeed.

As these statements suggest, the personal theories—or simply the preferences—of the people who have charge of organizing courses in freshman English determine the nature of the course; and what goes by the name of freshman composition on one campus may bear little resemblance to a course of the same name on another. The course may be based on any of the following, or on innumerable combinations of them:

1. Traditional grammar, usage, and mechanics (punctuation, spelling), often with the familiar exercises in sentence diagraming
2. The "new grammar"—structural linguistics
3. Literature, organized by major types, by major figures, by restriction to a certain period such as twentieth century, or by restriction to someone's list of Great Books of the Western World

4. Rhetoric of various kinds, from the classical theory of Aristotle and Quintilian to the familiar nineteenth-century systems of paragraph development and "forms of discourse"

5. Logic, in amounts ranging from only a day or two spent discussing fallacies to book-length treatments that dominate an entire semester's work

6. Semantics of various kinds and according to various prophets

7. The communication process and the mass media

8. Public speaking

9. Propaganda analysis

10. A kind of watered-down social science survey based on collections of essays drawn for the most part from current magazines

And then there are the maverick courses—sometimes both interesting and substantial—that do not fit into any of these categories, such as the course at a distinguished men's liberal arts college that, at least until recently, required each student to buy a box of colored crayons to use in preparing some of the assignments.

Usually it is hard to detect much evidence of clear progression in the freshman English course. The second semester is likely to be either a totally different course from the first—a course in lyric poetry, for example, or one in the short story, following one in usage and expository writing—or a mere repetition of the first semester distinguished only by the requirement of a long paper. Often there appears to be little real difference between the kind of content and writing assignments found in the freshman course and those with which the student has grown all too familiar during the three or four years before he entered college—topic sentences and the uses of the apostrophe, sentence outlines and subject-verb agreement, papers to be written on "My Favorite Teacher," "A Happy Vacation," "My Most Embarrassing Moment."

Quality of Teaching. Although there are exceptions, especially in smaller colleges, the freshman course is most commonly assigned to graduate students who teach part-time while working toward an advanced degree and to junior instructors newly out of graduate school or recouping their finances by a few years of full-time teaching between the master's degree and the doctorate. The latter are found most commonly where no advanced degree in English is offered. The former flourish at almost every university that offers a doctorate in English and at many institutions where only a master's degree is available. The plan is attractive to the administration because it means substantially cheaper teaching for the largest course on the campus. It is attractive to the senior professors in the English department because it means customers for the graduate courses that they want to teach. (At more than one institution these part-time teachers are almost the only customers for the graduate courses.) And it is attractive to the graduate students themselves because it offers them a kind of subsidy without which most of them would be unable to seek advanced degrees.

Some of these teachers are enthusiastic, experienced, expert; more are bored or resentful, lack previous teaching experience, are ill-informed on what they are supposed to teach, particularly on language and composition, and are teaching with little supervision or guidance. Part of the trouble is the sheer size of the operation, especially in the state universities. Last year, for example, one such institution had a freshman class of 7,500, which was divided into sections of approximately twenty-five students each. This meant some 300 sections of freshman English to be taught. All of them were taught by graduate students since the university could not afford to hire enough experienced and expert teachers for so large a program, even if such people were available in the necessary numbers—and of course they are not.

Another part of the difficulty is the lack of status that the freshman course has long suffered from. On many campuses freshman English has been a subcollegiate course, one that is clearly more appropriate to the high school than to an institution of higher education. In intellectual rigor it has too often been inferior to other freshman courses. Most English departments have regarded it as a kind of therapy that they perform without enthusiasm, and they have made it into a narrowly practical how-to-do-it course with few if any intellectual pretensions. In many universities that are unable to impose entrance requirements, the freshman English course has frankly been viewed by administrative officials as a means of weeding out academic undesirables who cannot be prevented from enrolling. Because of the kind of course that freshman English has become as a result of these circumstances, the best minds in the profession have rarely concerned themselves with it or its problems. Few first-rate men have taken the trouble to write textbooks for freshman English. A great deal of research has been done on aspects of the course but almost invariably by professors of education and their graduate students, hardly ever by people whose primary interest is English. It is seldom a course that most teachers—even most graduate students—look forward to teaching, but instead one that they merely endure and too often do not give their best efforts to.

But much of the poor teaching that one so often finds in freshman English is less the result of inexperience and indifference than of inadequate professional preparation—as indeed it is in the high schools also. The blame for this state of affairs must rest squarely with the college departments of English that have given these teachers their undergraduate and graduate education. Preoccupied with the study of literature, English departments seldom require the future English teacher—high school or college—to take courses that would give him a genuine professional competence in teaching either language or composition; yet it has been estimated that for the first six years of his career the college English teacher will find that 90 per cent of his teaching will consist of classes of freshman English in which he is supposed to teach both language and writing.[4] Missing from the usual English curriculum for the prospective teacher of English are courses in advanced composition, history of the English language, the modern study of English structure, rhetorical theory, English prose style, logic, semantics. The curriculum is almost entirely literary, with the result that the young teacher of freshman English is ill-prepared for the job he is asked to do and pines for the day when he can teach the literature for which his studies have qualified him. The effect of this attitude on the quality of teaching and on the morale of teacher and students can be surmised.

Quality of Textbooks. Freshman textbooks in many fields could stand considerable improving, but those for freshman English courses—in particular, the handbooks and the books of readings—are, as a class, likely to be among the poorest, the least scholarly, that the student will encounter. There are some good books among them, of course, but they are the exceptions in what has become a fantastically overcrowded field.

[4] *The Basic Issues in the Teaching of English,* presented by members of the American Studies Association, College English Association, Modern Language Association, and National Council of Teachers of English, 1959, p. 12.

Most handbooks are deficient both in their view of language and in their theory of rhetoric. The attitude toward language that one finds in most of the current handbooks is still largely prescriptive, though it is true that this emphasis has lessened over the past ten years. Few books, however, have yet tried to present to the college freshman even a small part of the new knowledge about language that has revolutionized the serious study of this subject in the last several decades. As for rhetoric, the majority of handbooks present a desiccated rhetorical doctrine that has probably done a good deal more over the years to hinder good writing than to foster it—the position of the topic sentence and mechanical rules for developing expository paragraphs, sets of critical abstractions which the student is urged to apply to his paragraphs and themes like a foot rule to a piece of lumber, injunctions about length of sentences (not too long, not too short), and the importance of figures of speech.

The books of readings, used presumably for analysis and imitation but actually serving more often than not merely as springboards for discussions of things in general, are a phenomenon peculiar to freshman English. Again, it must be admitted that some of these books have been put together with intelligence and taste, but the overwhelming majority of them are cut-and-paste affairs that can ill sustain a course of true college grade. Typical section headings in one of these books include "The College Scene," "The Relations of God to Man," "The Individual and the State," "The Meaning of America," "Freedom of Expression," "Man and Woman," "The Art of Living," and "Science and the Future." The last of these, in the volume quoted from, is followed by the parenthetical subheading "Where is science taking us?" The answer presumably is contained in the forty pages that follow, in which an article on detergents is sandwiched between Herodotus's explanation of why the Nile overflows and a selection by C. P. Snow.

The overabundance of textbooks for freshman English has already been mentioned, but it will be of some interest to spell out the extent of this abundance a little more exactly. As part of the analysis of freshman programs, a list was made of all the textbooks that were required. Seventy-six of the ninety-eight course descriptions specified texts. Leaving out dictionaries, complete literary works, and the so-called "controlled research" or "source" books, the list included the following:

57 different books of readings (two-thirds in use at only
   one college)
24 handbooks (half in use at only one college)
12 workbooks (all but one in use at different colleges)
 4 handbook-reader combinations
35 literary anthologies
22 miscellaneous textbooks

Included in the miscellaneous group were four research-paper manuals, three books on linguistics, two on public speaking, two on logic and semantics, two on logic alone, two on developing reading skill, a style sheet, a glossary of literary terms, a book on how to write technical reports, a pamphlet on spelling, another on using dictionaries, a massive cultural, intellectual, and social history of the United States, and finally something called *30 Days to a More Powerful Vocabulary*.

From the fact that at seventy-six colleges and universities fifty-seven different freshman essay anthologies are being used, one can draw a number of possible conclusions: (1) Many of these books are so nearly alike that it matters little which one is used. (2) Fads and novelties affect choice of these books as much as they do choice of women's hats. (3) Local authorship plays a large part in the decision to adopt one of the books, since two-thirds of them are used at only a single school on the list, often where one of the authors is employed. (4) The glut of these books, all produced by presumably busy scholars, suggests that the job of putting one of them together is considerably less burdensome than the writing of most other kinds of books. (5) Fifty-seven different books of readings for what in theory is the same course suggests a degree of uncertainty about the aims, methods, and proper content of the course. Perhaps none of these interpretations is entirely true, but none is wholly false either. Certainly there is an extraordinary number of these collections on the market, and they come and go with extraordinary rapidity.

After this survey of the difficulties under which the freshman English course labors, it will be useful to look more closely at the course in its various forms to get some notion of the specific policies that govern the work done in it. The practice is now almost universal of making some provision to segregate students in this course by their presumed ability in English composition. Since the course patterns that result from such a policy differ considerably from one another, it will be best to look separately at those for poorly prepared students, for superior students, and for the majority of students who fall into neither of these groups.

Remedial Courses. The number of colleges and universities offering remedial English courses has dropped sharply in the last several years. Though the trend may be said to have been started by the widely publicized decision of the University of Illinois to drop its own course, it has been reinforced by the pressure of rising enrollments and by the recent national concern for raising educational standards at all levels. A little more than half of the ninety-five schools whose freshman English programs were studied had no such course on their books in 1960–1961, and at least three of those that did dropped the course the next year. Probably no more than 40 per cent of the schools still offer the course; often, though not always, these schools are located in states where legal requirements prevent selective admission. One university in the South frankly calls its course "subcollegiate" and says that the main object of the course "is to teach high school English to weak college students." It underlines the point by requiring a high school textbook of grammar and rhetoric. A few schools that do not have a formal remedial course maintain "writing clinics" which the poorest students are either required or invited to attend in order to get special help. Increasingly, students appear to be put on their own in such matters: "This help is available; it's up to you whether to take advantage of it."

Of those schools that still offer a remedial course, about two-thirds give it without credit, and nearly all the others hedge the credit about with some kind of restriction. In some places the credit does not count toward graduation, and thus a student taking the course has a three-hour deficiency to make up. In others, the student is required to attend class five hours a week but gets only three credits.

Two-thirds of the schools that give the course offer it as a part of the regular curriculum, available during school hours and taught by members of the English department (though nearly always graduate students or junior instructors). No fee is charged. The others have removed it from the English department entirely and offer it, for a special fee, by extension (in the evening or by correspondence) or in the summer session only.

Students are assigned to remedial courses on the basis of standardized objective placement tests, often backed up by one or more compositions. Most schools have provisions for correcting errors in placement, either upward or downward, on the evidence of the first two or three themes written in whichever course a student has been assigned to. The percentage of students put in remedial courses varies widely, from 40 or 45 per cent at three universities on the list to only 5 or 7 per cent at other institutions. The mean is about 15 per cent.

The content of these courses is, as would be expected, mainly drill on grammar, usage, punctuation, spelling, and elementary rhetoric—sentence structure, the simpler kinds of paragraph structure. Workbooks are commonly used, often taking up more time in the course than practice in actual composition does. Papers are customarily assigned at the rate of one a week, though written exercises of one kind or another may come more often. The papers are nearly always short—no more than a page or two—and often may consist of only a single paragraph. Topics generally are pointed toward the student's own experience and call for simple narrative or expository treatment. A large proportion of the writing is done in class, sometimes all of it. The reason seems to be compounded of a desire to give more individual help to the student as he is composing and an anxiety to be sure that the student is doing his own work.

Provisions for the Superior Student. As college English departments have shown less and less concern for the needs of the dullest and most poorly prepared students, they have taken a sharply increased interest in the needs of those who are brightest and best prepared. More than two-thirds of the ninety-five colleges were making some special provision for superior students in 1960–1961; and since this trend is still on the rise, there is no doubt that the proportion is even higher now. Among those institutions that apparently were not making some effort to accommodate the usual freshman English requirement to the needs of the bright student were three small and highly selective colleges that do not teach freshman English at all; at most of the others, special treatment for individuals is possible through the Advanced Placement Program.

The particular arrangements made for these students take many forms. In some institutions a few students may be totally exempted from any requirement in freshman English, though they will usually be required or encouraged to elect one or more advanced courses in English. In many places bright students are exempted from a part of the normal requirement—the first term usually—then either made to take the rest of the regular sequence or, more commonly, put in an accelerated course that combines in one term the work of two. Sometimes a grade of A or B in the accelerated course will confer double credit; more commonly, students satisfactorily passing the course are asked to elect another English course, nearly always a more advanced one in literature. Some colleges and universities do not exempt students at all but instead put them either in homogeneously grouped sections of the regular course in which the standards have been set higher than in the regular sections or in a special full-length sequence with different textbooks—new courses, really, more challenging to good students than the regular courses would be. These sections often are quite small, a dozen or fifteen students.[5]

The students thus singled out for special attention are identified in several ways. Colleges and universities that use the College Board tests are likely to rely principally on scores for the Verbal Aptitude Test and the English Composition Achievement Test, together with the "Writing Sample" when it is available. The decision may be shaded with such other factors as high school grades, an evaluation of the high school itself, and predictions of a student's academic success made by high school teachers and principals. Institutions not affiliated with the College Board use a variety of other objective tests, sometimes locally developed. These tests may be supplemented by a short theme. A few schools exempt students from the first-term course solely on test and other data assembled before actual enrollment. Most require eligible students to take a special proficiency test and to pass it with distinction. This examination is usually an impromptu composition on a topic demanding rather lengthy and complex treatment. At still other institutions, students are not exempted from the first course but may be exempted from the second on the basis of grades earned in the first—usually A or B. There are great differences from school to school in the percentage of students for whom these special arrangements are made. At some, as many as a fourth of the freshman class are exempted from the first course; at others, as few as 3 or 4 per cent.

[5] For a fuller discussion of exemption policy and procedures, see Appendix A, pp. 157–163.

In the special sections and courses, sometimes the same textbooks are used as in the regular classes, but the level of class discussion, the quantity of reading, and the quality of writing are adjusted to the greater potential of superior students. Usually, however, some or all of the texts will be different from those used in the other classes—longer, more difficult, often more of them.

The great majority of these special classes have a pronounced literary bias, usually with considerable writing done in connection with the study of literary texts. Sometimes literature is frankly in the foreground—courses in literature, with occasional assignments in writing; other courses claim to be primarily ones in composition, with literature read mainly to serve the purposes of instruction in writing. When the pattern specifies more than one course, the literary emphasis is likely to be stronger in the later course or courses of the sequence, which sometimes become purely courses in literature, with examinations the only writing.

Perhaps most commonly the literature content comprises a survey of major types, though a sort of indiscriminate "great books" or world literature emphasis is often found. One Midwestern university has prepared several lists of six or eight paperbacks, each list dealing with a common theme ("The Dead Sea Scrolls," "Freud and His Critics"). Instructors of the special sections choose one of the groups of titles as the reading for their classes.

The writing in these special courses is usually expository, if the term is construed broadly to include the kind of analytical and evaluative writing that arises from the close study of literature. The total amount of writing required is usually greater than in the regular courses. Papers are likely to be fewer but longer—800 to 1,000 words rather than 500 to 600. At least one unusually long paper is a normal feature of each special course. This paper, which may range anywhere from 1,200 to 5,000 words, is based either on one of the many "controlled research" books or on library investigation.

The Standard Program. Depending on how many students a particular college separates from the top and bottom of the pile, the standard freshman English program may enroll anywhere from 55 to 97 per cent of the freshman class. For the ninety-five schools studied, the mean is about 75 per cent.

The primary emphasis in the first course of the standard program is on expository reading and writing; better than four out of five of the colleges on the list exhibit this emphasis. Early in the term it is a fairly common practice to require some reading of biography, autobiography, and description and to ask the student to write a few narrative or descriptive papers based on personal experience, but this work is usually intended only as a preliminary to the study of exposition.

Except for a few highly individual programs, the remaining fifth emphasize the study of literature, with writing assignments growing out of this study. The literature is most commonly organized by types; the writing is analysis and criticism of individual works. With a few exceptions the colleges where this literary emphasis appears in the first term are those with rigorous standards for admission— the Ivy League and a number of small, highly selective liberal arts colleges. One explanation for this tendency, and the one most likely to be advanced publicly, is that most students at such schools are better prepared in English than the average entering freshman and can safely forego systematic instruction in the mechanics of composition and the rhetoric of expository prose. This explanation is by no means irrelevant, but certainly another to be considered is that many of these colleges have a long tradition of belletristic study in the freshman course that they are reluctant to depart from.

Though the main focus in the first term is generally on the reading and writing of exposition, a number of other concerns appear often enough to deserve mention. One of these is the familiar "review of fundamentals," a survey of the conventions of grammar, usage, and punctuation that the student has suffered through annually from the seventh grade on. At some colleges the "review" may last all term; at others it comes in the first weeks. This feature of the freshman course appears to be declining, however, especially where enrollment pressures have become acute or where there has been an appreciable rise in the quality of students admitted. At such colleges the level of performance expected of students has been raised, with the result that class discussion of elementary errors in correctness is being drastically reduced and often eliminated. Increasingly, students are left to decide for themselves how much reviewing they must do to correct this kind of mistake. The errors in their compositions are identified by the teacher, but unless a certain error is being made by a considerable number of students in the class, it is not discussed during class time; the student is referred to a handbook for enlightenment or (in chronic cases) to a writing clinic. In effect, many college English departments are now saying—and meaning it—that matters of this sort are not a proper subject for collegiate instruction and must be learned before the student enters college.

Another concern of the first term of freshman English is the serious study not just of so-called "functional grammar" but of language itself, especially English. The study is justified not primarily as a means of improving writing but rather for its value in a scheme of liberal education. About a tenth of the courses examined included some work of this sort, often extending over several weeks. Another discipline figuring in the courses of the first term is logic, which appears in about one course out of eight. Semantics is a third, appearing about as often as logic but taking up much less room in the course now than when it was at the height of its vogue fifteen or twenty years ago.

In the second course of the freshman English sequence, the pattern in colleges on the semester system is likely to differ from that of those on the quarter system. Under either plan this one year of English will be, for most students, the only required work in the subject. The second semester is, then, more often than not the terminal course, and with this in mind a little over two-thirds of the English departments operating on the semester plan require the reading of literature in this term to ensure that all students will have at least a minimal exposure. The writing tends mainly to be analysis and criticism of the literature.

In colleges that are on the quarter system, which provides three terms instead of two, only a fourth of the programs specify this kind of reading and writing for the second course. The most prominent emphasis in the second-quarter course is on logic, particularly in relation to argumentative and expository reading and writing. (Only about a fifth of the colleges on the semester system have this emphasis in the second semester, though two of the three that require a third semester of English include logic in that course.)

Another kind of emphasis that can be observed in the second-term courses is advanced rhetoric, usually in conjunction with a more sophisticated study of exposition than was found in the first term. Of the colleges on the quarter system, roughly one out of five has this pattern; of those on the semester plan, one out of ten.

In the third-quarter course, more than half of the colleges using this plan specify literary readings (with related writing), since this is usually the terminal course of the sequence. The others show a great variety—mass media, style, semantics, logic, exposition, American civilization. Some writing, usually expository, is customary regardless of course content.

In colleges and universities on the semester plan, the amount of writing varies in the first semester from 3,600 words to 10,000. The first of these figures comes from an Ivy League university which asks its freshmen for three 1,200-word papers in its one-semester course (it is a course in literature). The second comes from a college on the West Coast which requires its freshmen to write 20,000 words in two semesters of English composition. The mean figure for the institutions on the list is about 6,000 words in eleven themes. These papers average 500 to 550 words, with those written in class a little shorter and those outside a little longer. In the second semester about ten papers are written, but since one of these is usually a "long" paper, the total number of words written in this term approaches 8,000.

Where the quarter system is in effect, about seven themes are written in each of the three terms. The length of papers averages 500 to 550 words in the first and third quarters but 700 in the second, when it is usual to require a longer paper. (Only a few colleges ask for another long paper in the third quarter.)

A few schools on the list require a long paper in the first term; it is rarely a research paper but instead an extended narrative or exposition of the same general kind that the student has been writing earlier. In the second term three-fourths of the freshman programs require a long paper, and a little more than half of these ask for the usual "library" paper. Most of the others base the assignment on one of the many "controlled research" books, which ease the strain on library facilities and reduce the danger of plagiarism. It is interesting that about a fourth of the programs do not require any kind of long paper. The syllabus of one state university tells instructors that they may assign papers over 1,000 words long if they wish, but they should do so "only after the most careful consideration. Almost all detected plagiarism in English 4 themes occurs in papers over 1,000 words long. . . ."

The great majority of young people entering college each fall can expect to do a lot of impromptu writing in their freshman English classes. A few colleges, in fact, require all themes to be written in class, and many require half. The mean would probably be at least a third. The few colleges that do not insist on one or more impromptu papers are generally those with very selective admission policies, but even in the Ivy League class themes are not unknown. These papers always count more heavily than those written outside of class. The explanation is that class papers are the only ones that the instructor can be absolutely sure are the result of every student's unaided labors. A number of colleges require the last two or three papers of the course to be written in class; the student must get passing grades on these themes to pass the course.

In spite of the pressure of rising enrollments, themes are usually marked and graded by a student's own instructor rather than by a theme reader (even though the instructor may often be a graduate student just beginning to teach). This situation may not last. Several colleges and universities are now using readers for themes. The growth of the "lay reader" plan in high schools may soon encourage college administrators to extend it to freshman English courses as an economy measure: though graduate students can scarcely be called expensive labor, housewives cost even less.

A Note on the Communication Course. The special variety of freshman English course called "Communication" (sometimes "Basic Communication") is distinguished from the usual composition course by its primary focus on the process of communication, often in a fairly sophisticated way, and on the four "communication skills," reading, writing, speaking, and listening. The typical course of this sort is oriented more toward the social sciences than toward the humanities. The orientation of the composition course is the reverse. The communication course is concerned more with the accuracy of verbal expression and less with its esthetic qualities. The composition course tends to be equally concerned with both. Linguistics, semantics, logic, persuasion and argument, group dynamics, and the mass media are all likely to be studied in a communication course. Required reading seems rarely to be literary but consists instead of books and articles on language and communication and of newspapers and magazines studied as examples of the mass media.

Fifteen years ago communication courses were springing up

everywhere. By 1948 there were 200 in existence. Today their vogue has largely passed. Most colleges and universities that once had them have abandoned them entirely; some of the rest appear to be choking them off with various administrative restrictions; a few others have kept the name but have dropped attempts to give instruction in speaking and listening and have in effect made the course into simply another variety of composition course.

Among the ninety-five institutions on the list, only six retain full-fledged communication courses that offer instruction and practice in reading, writing, speaking, and listening. Three of them, part of a "general college" pattern within state universities, exist alongside much larger, conventional programs in composition. Three others, also part of a general education curriculum, seem to have maintained their vigor undiminished, at least partly as a result of a considerable degree of administrative independence that they have enjoyed.

Rarely, an otherwise conventional composition program will make a nod toward the claims of spoken English by requiring one or two short (3-minute) speeches during the year. But for the most part, except for the surviving communication courses, freshman English programs do not attempt to give formal instruction in oral discourse.

The most exciting educational development of the last half dozen years has been the widespread effort to improve the quality of instruction in several of the basic academic subjects, mainly by identifying and concentrating more directly upon their central principles and by bringing their content more nearly into line with current knowledge of the particular disciplines. On the strength of the analysis just concluded, one finds little evidence that the people who plan and run freshman English courses, or those who write textbooks for these courses, have been at all conscious of this movement or of its bearing on their own concerns. Most of them are still doing business in the same old way at the same old stand. Freshman English in the nation's colleges and universities is now so confused, so clearly in need of radical and sweeping reforms, that college English departments can continue to ignore the situation only at their increasing peril.

Chapter 2

English Composition at Dartmouth College

THE FRESHMAN ENGLISH COURSES AT DARTMOUTH

After the general survey just presented of the many varieties of freshman English courses and of the conditions that prevail in them, it will now be profitable to look closely at one particular freshman English program, that at Dartmouth College. Dartmouth cannot, it is true, be called a typical American college, though it is typical of a certain important kind of American college. It is, in the first place, a restricted-enrollment college, accepting only a small fraction of the young men who apply for admission; and in general it is only the better students who choose to apply to this kind of college. The average student taking freshman English at Dartmouth is noticeably superior both in intelligence and in preparation to his counterpart at less favored colleges and universities. And since the size of the freshman class is strictly controlled, being held to almost the same figure year after year, the English department is protected from the pressures that elsewhere are forcing heavy increases in class size and teacher load or are otherwise lowering the quality of teaching in this course.

Since Dartmouth does not offer graduate degrees in English, there are no graduate students to whom the teaching of freshman English can be relegated. The Dartmouth English staff is composed entirely of full-time teachers with a high degree of professional competence, educated at the best universities and already experienced in teaching before they are hired. Moreover, the lack of graduate courses at Dartmouth has meant that undergraduate teaching enjoys a status that it often lacks in universities, where many

27

teachers regard it without enthusiasm and aspire to teach only graduate students. At Dartmouth the freshman English courses are taught by all members of the department and are thought to be worthy of the best efforts of the staff.

Though freshman English at Dartmouth may not be typical in enjoying so much happier circumstances than the course often does elsewhere, this fact alone makes it worth a close look, for it is freed from some of the inhibiting conditions that often prevent English teachers elsewhere from doing as good a job as they would like in the freshman course. There are other reasons also why the Dartmouth course deserves attention. One is that although the fortunate circumstances that it enjoys are not widely typical, they are not unique. A significant number of other colleges and universities, especially in the East but not there alone, bear a generic resemblance to Dartmouth and in varying degrees benefit from the same kind of circumstances. In some respects (though not all) these institutions are the bellwethers of American higher education, so that developments in their curricula often are significant to other kinds of colleges and universities as well. Another reason is that although the average freshman at Dartmouth may be brighter and better prepared academically than the average freshman in most other colleges and universities, these institutions enroll many bright and well-prepared young people. At almost any state university, for example, there are some freshmen who are the equals of the best that attend Dartmouth. The proportion of these superior students appears to be rising, and the institutions at which they enroll are taking an increasingly keen interest in their special educational needs. In this respect, then, an English program suitable for the kind of student who comes to Dartmouth should be suitable also for a significant number of students at less selective institutions, and there is a clear trend in these institutions to make special provisions for unusually able students.

Still another reason why an examination of Dartmouth's freshman English courses should have more than local interest is that the particular emphasis which distinguishes these courses at Dartmouth is one that is now prominent in a wide variety of colleges and universities and seems likely to become increasingly widespread in the next few years. That is, the Dartmouth freshman English program is a striking example of that particular variety that is centered on the study of standard literature, with writing assignments growing out of this study; an examination of the Dartmouth courses ought therefore to shed light on a significant philosophy of teaching freshman English, as well as provide an opportunity to consider problems that are common to all varieties of the course. Finally, the principles of good writing, and most of the problems that one must deal with in teaching good writing, are essentially the same no matter where the subject is taught. The job of teaching composition to students at a land-grant university and the job of teaching it to students at Dartmouth College have more points of similarity than of difference. It is the same English language that is being put to use, the same rhetorical principles, the same principles of orderly thinking.

Since 1958 Dartmouth has operated on a term instead of a semester plan, with three 10-week terms occupying the usual academic year. The freshman English requirement consists of two term courses, English 1 and English 2. By action of the faculty several years ago, 25 per cent of each freshman class is exempted from English 1 on the basis of test scores and other predictive data available at the time of admission. A very few students (so far, less than a dozen each year) are exempted from both courses on the basis either of Advanced Placement credit or of performance on a special examination given by the English department to roughly the top 10 per cent of each freshman class just before the fall term opens.

English 1, which is entitled "Literature and Composition for Freshmen," is described as follows in the College catalog:

> The course aims, through the study and discussion of selections from Shakespeare and Milton, to increase the student's capacity for enjoying and appreciating great literature. It also aims to develop clear thinking and correct and clear expression. Frequent themes are required, and no student will receive credit for the course until he has demonstrated his ability to write satisfactorily.

Notice that the principal objective of this course is literary appreciation; subsidiary aims are "clear thinking" and "correct and clear expression."

In practice, the reading in this course consists of three plays of Shakespeare, usually chosen to represent a variety of types—comedy, history, tragedy—and Milton's *Paradise Lost*. A typical selection of plays would be *King Lear*, *The Tempest*, and *Henry IV, Part I*. The particular plays are changed frequently, but *Paradise Lost* has been taught in freshman English at Dartmouth for many years. Some teachers find time to assign and discuss the entire poem; others —perhaps half the staff—cover about three-fourths of it.

Normally seven papers (plus an hour exam) are required in English 1. The papers average 700 or 800 words each. The policy of the department is to require critical and analytical essays based on the literature being studied, though the policy is not uniformly followed. Examples of the usual kind of topic would be "The Role of Enobarbus in *Antony and Cleopatra*," "Richard III—'Hell's Black Intelligencer,'" "Who Was at Fault: Adam or Eve?" Sometimes topics take a different twist, when students use the literature as a springboard for general philosophical speculation: "People Like It" (an essay on evil) or "Steps of Honor" (a discussion of honor, using Brutus as a point of departure). Some teachers habitually, and others occasionally, permit informal personal essays on a variety of topics: "Casting for Fresh Water Bass," "The Bearded Parasite" (strictures on beatniks), "Is the American Automobile Too Large?" and "Has College Spirit Faded?" Occasionally, narrative or descriptive sketches are permitted; rarely, such things as dramatic skits or letters to hypothetical editors and congressmen.

Although these themes are assigned at regular intervals, marked by the teacher, and revised by the student, the study of literature dominates the course. The organization of English 1 is determined not by linguistic or rhetorical considerations but (loosely) by the literary works being read—the Shakespearean plays first, with the least difficult usually beginning the course, and *Paradise Lost* at the end. Departmental policy specifies that several class hours in English 1 be designated as "composition meetings" at which writing problems will be discussed, but the rule is not generally followed. A conventional handbook of grammar, rhetoric, and usage is one of the required texts, though it is used only for reference.

Because classes are small (as freshman English classes go) and because of a long tradition at Dartmouth of individual instruction, teachers generally have at least one conference a term with each student, and with many they have more than one. "Problem" students sometimes have what amounts almost to a tutorial arrangement. In these conferences the most frequent subject of discussion is the student's themes and the difficulties that are apparent in them. In so far as writing is explicitly taught in English 1, it is taught in these conferences.

English 2 is a strikingly unusual course to find in the freshman year. Called "Freshman Seminar in English," it is described as follows in the catalog:

> The course is designed to provide the student the maximum opportunity for responsible, independent study, and to offer him experience in the use of the library. Each section may be divided into two seminar groups. Topics for study are chosen by the instructor (e.g., an important figure or theme in English or American literature, representative figures of a period, a literary genre, or a major work). The seminars meet as directed by the instructor, normally once or twice a week. Short papers on work in progress and at least one long paper are required. Each instructor gives a two-hour final examination.

Several things are worth noting in this description. First, the aims do not include gaining a familiarity with a particular body of literature studied in all sections of the course; instead, literature is specified as the content, but the choice of literature is up to the instructor, who has only general criteria to guide him. Second, the principal objectives are to introduce the student to independent study and to teach him how to use the library. In practice, these mean instruction in the technique of library research. Third, it is noteworthy that, unlike English 1, this course does not list improvement of writing as an explicit aim, though from the fact that a long paper and several short ones are required one may assume that it is an implicit aim. (The total wordage required is approximately the same in both courses.) Finally, although the course is termed a seminar, not all teachers divide their classes into two small groups of eight or nine students each and run the groups as true seminars. Frequently a teacher will keep the class together and meet it four times a week just as he would an English 1 class.

The particular topic chosen by the instructor for study in his section of English 2 must be approved by the Steering Committee for Freshman English. The present policy of the committee is to require that the literature specified for a given topic meet two of three criteria: It must deal with a major literary genre (tragedy, satire, epic, comedy), include significant works by at least two major figures in English or American literature, or include a major work written before 1800. Among the topics approved in the last few years have been fairly conventional ones, such as "The Concept of Tragedy," "Hardy and Conrad," and "Literature of the 1920s, English and American." Others, however, have included "Initiation as a Theme in Fiction," " 'Nature' and 'Convention' in Selected Works of English Literature," "The Irrational in Literature," "The Spiritual Journey," and "The Fall of Man." In all sections, students choose a particular research topic rising from the general subject of the course and do subsidiary reading as they prepare the long paper which presents the results of their research.

Besides the long paper, which is supposed to run from 1,500 to 2,000 words, students are asked to write three or four short papers (700 to 800 words) based on the general topic that they have chosen to investigate. Thus a student may write short papers on "Responsibility in *Light in August* and *Pudd'nhead Wilson*" or "Structure: Its Purposes in the Opening Scenes of *The White Devil*," while at work on a long paper dealing with Faulkner or Webster. But as in English 1, not all instructors follow the official policy. Other topics may include "The Purpose of a Hobby," "The Development of an Opinion" (a discussion of a "social problems" course taken in high school), "The Unskilled Worker and Life," and "Let's Clean Polluted Waters"—even though the literature being studied may be the poetry of the seventeenth century, a selection of English novels, or several works by major dramatists. The long papers are, however, nearly always based directly on some aspect of the announced theme of the course—"The Theme of the Artist as Exile with Reference to W. Somerset Maugham's *Moon and Sixpence* and P. Wyndham Lewis's *Tarr*," or "The Ethical Systems Embodied in Shaftesbury's *Characteristics* and Mandeville's *Fable of the Bees*, as Compared with That of Pope's *Essay on Man*," or "A Comparison of the Resurrection of Christ and Pagan Resurrection Myths" (in a course studying the Bible as literature).

Writing is taught in English 2 much as it is in English 1: The teacher assigns and marks the papers, the student revises them, and occasionally teacher and student have a conference during which writing problems may be discussed. No "composition meetings" are specified. Except for the instruction in the use of the library and in research technique, English 2 is a highly specialized course in literature with several related assignments in writing.

Regarded either as freshman courses in English or as courses in "freshman English," English 1 and 2 at Dartmouth have undeniable attractions. Perhaps the two most impressive things about them are that they are genuinely college-level courses and that they are genuinely courses in English. In the light of what often goes by the name of freshman English elsewhere, these are no slight advantages to boast of. The Dartmouth courses are solid, stimulating, intellectually respectable—as indeed they should be to deserve a place among the curricular offerings of a distinguished college.

However, in evaluating these courses for the purposes of this study, which is concerned principally with the teaching of writing, it is important to bear in mind that composition is almost never taught directly in class in English 1 and 2. Class time is spent analyzing and discussing works of literature that are considered to be worth studying for their own sake—a view that no English teacher would want to quarrel with. This kind of activity is not completely irrelevant to instruction in composition. Any discussion that serves to reveal, even if indirectly, the principles of literary structure or effective word choice or sentence rhythm bears on the teaching of writing. An analysis of the speeches of Brutus and Antony over the body of the dead Caesar may open the student's eyes to the importance of adapting discourse to a particular audience. A study of Milton's use of alliteration in the account of Satan's expulsion from Heaven may help to make the student sensitive to the force of this device—and possibly aware of its dangers in less elevated composition. One might also expect that the student's ability to write would be enhanced to some extent by the forming and improving of his taste that an increasing familiarity with good literature ought to bring about.

The literary content of such courses as Dartmouth's English 1 and 2, besides being attractive in its own right, has still other advantages for the teaching of composition. The perennial problem of what to write about that has afflicted generations of composition students need not arise in such courses, for there is always the literature. When composition assignments are based on the literature, both reading and writing can benefit: The student has a copious supply of proper subjects for writing, and his understanding of what he has read will be deepened when he is forced to clarify and order his ideas so that he can get them down on paper. The student who writes a thoughtful essay discussing whether Shakespeare's *Julius Caesar* ought instead to have been entitled *Brutus* will be brought by this exercise closer to an accurate appreciation of the play.

The teacher, too, profits from such an arrangement, for he is pleased with what he is teaching and usually competent to teach it; it is likely to be the kind of work he is sincerely committed to, the kind for which his professional study has prepared him. He enjoys the satisfaction of knowing that he is not merely proofreading his students' papers for superficial errors but criticizing and evaluating them as compositions that are saying something about matters that he is competent to judge. (Compare the all-too-familiar plight of the freshman English teacher who in successive weeks must read themes on atomic warfare, penal reform, drug addiction, and extra-sensory perception.) [1] If a student has misinterpreted Milton's position on free will or ascribed to Shakespeare himself an opinion that the poet has assigned for dramatic purposes to a character in one of the plays, the teacher must be able to set him right. The teacher knows that it is fully as important for the student's development as a competent writer of expository prose that he learn to reason clearly and interpret accurately as that he use conventional spelling and end sentences with periods instead of commas.

---

[1] A newly founded state university is now offering its freshmen a course in "functional English" organized around the following questions: "How does one understand the physical universe?" "How is society organized?" "How does one examine his society, past and present?" "What is one's relationship to the past?" "How does one perceive beauty?" "What should be one's view of the supernatural?" "How does one escape from actuality?" "What can one aspire to in life?" Each of these questions is buttressed by subordinate ones. Under the first, for example, are the following: "The origin of the physical universe: how did it begin?" "How did the evolutionary idea develop?" "What is the effect of science on modern life?"

One can agree that a college student ought to seek answers to all these questions but still wonder why the freshman English course should be singled out as the place to seek them.

Other points can also be made in favor of Dartmouth's English 1 and 2 as courses in which some effort is being made to teach writing, even if not explicitly in the classroom. One is that the staff is conscientious in assigning the full amount of writing specified by departmental policy, thus ensuring the practice without which all other instruction in composition is useless. This quantity of writing is encouraged by the favorable conditions of class size and teacher load that prevail at Dartmouth. Most other colleges and universities in the country are struggling desperately, in the face of mushrooming enrollments and a dwindling supply of qualified teachers, to maintain a semblance of quality in the teaching of this course, keeping the size of sections within reason and the number of sections assigned a given teacher within the bounds of human endurance. It appears to be a losing fight so far, with class size and teacher load rising steadily in many colleges, and closed-circuit television, large lecture sections, and theme readers burgeoning in others. At Dartmouth, where classes of English 1 and 2 never exceed twenty students and where two 4-hour sections are a full load, the problem simply does not exist. Teachers can and do mark papers with care, check the papers when they are returned by the student to see that they have been satisfactorily revised, and schedule conferences with students who need additional help.

The Dartmouth English staff is composed entirely of experienced, highly educated teachers, who, as devoted and expert teachers of literature, are entirely competent to judge whether a student has read and interpreted the literature accurately. They are also expert judges of student writing. They do not, it is true, agree perfectly on all details of composition; neither an English faculty, however competent, nor any other group can do that. But they are in substantial agreement on serious errors and principal virtues in student writing and, in general, on the over-all quality of particular papers.

When to all these advantages is added the happy circumstance of highly superior freshmen (60 per cent in 1961–1962 from the top tenth of their high school graduating class, a median score of 635 on the College Board's SAT Verbal and 617 on the English Composition Achievement Test), many a hard-pressed teacher at a less favored college will exclaim that surely freshman English at Dartmouth is being taught in an ideal way to ideal students in ideal circumstances. Dartmouth's English 1 and 2 are good English courses;

one should make no mistake about that. And they are being well taught. The question is whether they are doing as good a job as they should of teaching writing, which is the purpose of their being required for all students.

Viewed as courses in which the teaching of writing is supposed to be a principal object, English 1 and 2 (and other freshman English courses with a similar literary bias) are open to a major criticism: Often they are not courses in writing at all but courses in literature with some (usually) related writing exacted at fairly regular intervals. Because of training and natural inclination, the great majority of English teachers are most contented when they are teaching literature. They take more pleasure in speculating about the *Ur-Hamlet* or discussing Milton's prosody than in analyzing an expository paragraph to determine its structure or explaining the rhetorical effect of balanced sentences. In spite of the many advantages of using literary readings in a freshman composition course, literature often is like the nose of the camel under the edge of the tent: in no time at all the camel takes over the whole tent.

Though a first-rate job of teaching literature is being done in the freshman English courses at Dartmouth, writing is being taught only incidentally. There is no class discussion of the rhetorical principles or the principles of inductive and deductive reasoning that underlie the kind of writing (expository) that the students are supposedly being taught to master. No attempt is made in either course to deduce these principles in an orderly way from the literature studied. The study of composition and the study of literature can profitably be related by showing how the principles of composition (that is, of logic, rhetoric, and English structure) are exemplified in particular literary works. But one may argue that if these principles are to affect student writing, they ought to be clearly identified and their relevance to the student's task demonstrated. The student must be able to recognize them and must understand them well enough so that he can generalize from them. One may honestly doubt whether it is enough to rely on osmosis, even with superior students.

Two additional criticisms can be directed specifically toward English 1, the course in which the most direct effort is made to teach students to write better. The first concerns the literature read in this course, which represents one kind of extreme to which the literary emphasis in freshman English courses may be pushed. Most such courses that use readings from standard literature offer a potpourri of works, usually organized by genre—short stories, lyric and narrative verse, several plays, a novel or two. But if one were to ask English teachers what authors they would most like to teach, given a better world, what ones would give them the greatest satisfaction to discuss in the classroom, Shakespeare and Milton would surely be high on the list. Such a choice is understandable, for we have no greater authors than these, none that present a greater challenge to the teacher. But it is pertinent to ask whether Shakespeare's plays and Milton's epic, masterworks though they are, are entirely appropriate to the task of teaching expository writing to freshmen. In the first place, they represent only two literary forms, drama and epic, yet the student is expected to develop skill in quite a different genre, the expository or critical essay. Second, both the plays and *Paradise Lost* are in verse, whereas it seems reasonable to argue that the student ought to have at least some prose models. Third, the works of both Shakespeare and Milton are written in language that, however inspired, is nevertheless the language of some three or three and a half centuries ago and therefore in some ways limited as a model for imitation.

This is not to say that works by Shakespeare and Milton should be banned from freshman English. But when the *only* reading is Shakespeare and Milton in a course that aims to develop and refine a student's command of expository prose, or even when the only reading is imaginative literature, the job of teaching expository writing seems to have been made considerably harder than it need be. It seems reasonable to believe that the writing might be more effectively taught if the reading were to include a generous amount of first-rate expository prose. Our literature is rich with possibilities: Mill, Emerson, Arnold, Thoreau, Hazlitt, Forster, to name only those who first come to mind.

The other criticism that can be made of English 1, as the course in which instruction in writing is an explicit aim, can nearly always be made of other freshman English courses that emphasize literature. It is that no direct effort is made in it to teach the student anything about language in general or the English language in particular, the instrument over which he is expected to perfect his control. It is improbable that virtuosity in diagraming sentences or drawing up paradigms of English verbs will make anyone a better writer; experiments over the last fifty years, in fact, have suggested that mastery of such skills has no perceptible effect on the ability to write with fluency, correctness, and vigor. What is being suggested here is not just a knowledge of traditional "workbook" grammar—the eight parts of speech, the four kinds of sentences, the three types of dependent clauses—though a knowledge of this kind of grammar is better than no knowledge of grammar at all. Nor is it just a knowledge of the rules for conventional correctness that is being recommended—remembering to write "different from" instead of "different than," to prefer "the reason is that" to "the reason is because," and to split an infinitive only in moments of crisis. Correctness in writing is important; indeed, it is indispensable if one wishes to be thought an educated person. But it is essentially a superficial matter—language etiquette, good manners. It is not to be confused with a rounded study of language in general or of English, though it is part of such a study.

The sort of linguistic knowledge being suggested might include such things as the nature of language, the background and development of English, the principles of English structure, the relation of speech to writing, the bases of correctness in English. The amount of this material that could be included in most freshman courses is obviously limited, both by time and by the professional interests of most teachers. But even if only one or two of the topics could be studied, the student would have gained knowledge of intrinsic value about man's greatest and most characteristic invention; and, to the extent that he develops a fuller awareness of the nature of language, of its resources and limitations, it is possible that he might acquire a somewhat firmer and more discriminating command of the English tongue. And that is what training in English composition is supposed to foster.

It would be absurd to pretend that some study of language, rhetoric, and logic in a course that aims at improving the student's ability to write good exposition would work miracles and transform every freshman into an incipient Emerson. But the principles of English structure, of rhetoric, of logic are inevitably involved in the composition of clear, vigorous, expository prose. Not everyone needs to study these principles directly to master a good expository prose style; they can be learned intuitively, as many professional writers—and no doubt some college students—have learned them. But for most students, even most students at select colleges, it seems at least as reasonable to believe that studying these principles, and consciously practicing them under expert supervision, will have a favorable effect on the ability to write well-knit exposition as it is to believe that studying them will have no effect at all or that the effect is the same whether they are studied or not.

Like English 1, Dartmouth's English 2 is unusually attractive to teachers and might well be envied by English departments elsewhere. Not only does it give every teacher, regardless of rank, the opportunity to offer a seminar—in most English departments, a privilege usually reserved for a handful of senior professors—but it encourages each teacher to focus the course on his own field of specialization, whether metaphysical poetry, the realistic novel, or eighteenth-century satire. English 2 at its best is an impressive course to visit and can be a rewarding experience for teacher and student alike. But there are tendencies implicit in its premises that make one doubt whether a course of this type is suitable to serve as part of a required sequence in freshman English.

The first criticism that must be made of such a course as English 2 is based on the belief that a required freshman course in a basic academic subject such as English ought to have a certain degree of uniformity from section to section, else it ought not to be required. As English 2 is now constituted, it achieves such uniformity as it has through an agreement to concentrate on certain skills instead of on specific subject matter; its purposes are "to provide the student the maximum opportunity for responsible, independent study, and to offer him experience in the use of the library." To these purposes one may object that neither is a special prerogative of an English department, any more than of a history or a chemistry department; nor can an English department argue, as it can with respect to the teaching of writing, that although it does not bear the sole responsibility, it does have a special competence for the job that other departments lack. Meanwhile, this primary emphasis not on content but on what is really a kind of skill (research technique) means that the course has been cut loose from any common body of subject matter, except in so far as the entire corpus of English and American literature from Chaucer to the present day may be said to comprise one. The result is that the reading in individual sections of the course may vary enormously—from the novels of Hardy and Conrad to the poetry of Tennyson and Browning, from a selection of tragedies to a selection of modern short stories, from the poetry of Chaucer to that of T. S. Eliot.

When only such general guides are provided for the content of such a course, there is danger that individualism will become idiosyncrasy. One may agree that "Initiation as a Theme in Fiction" and "Shakespeare's London: 1599–1600" are both excellent topics for study, but the distance between them must be recognized.

A second criticism of this course is really an extension of the first: its excessive narrowness when viewed as a required course. The seminar plan of organization which underlies it requires a narrow focus on whatever subject is decided on, but one may question whether the freshman year is the proper time for such specialization. And the seminar plan itself is open to question when used for a freshman course to be taken by all students. It is not merely chance that has restricted seminars in American colleges and universities primarily to the graduate level, with a few open to juniors and seniors majoring in the subject in question and a very few to highly superior underclassmen enrolled in special honors programs. If a seminar is to deserve the name, the students in it must already have a large fund of general knowledge about the field being studied, as well as a certain amount of specialized knowledge; if they lack these qualifications, they cannot contribute usefully to the kind of discussion that is the lifeblood of a true seminar, nor can they profitably pursue the investigation of a special topic within the general field to which the seminar is restricted. The course under such circumstances is no longer a seminar. Considering the hit-and-miss experience that most students have with literature in high school, it is doubtful whether the great majority of freshmen, even at the most selective colleges, are prepared to cope successfully with a true seminar dealing with such topics as "The Hero and the Community" or "Some Metamorphoses of Satan and the Satanic in English and American Literature."

Other colleges, then, that might be tempted to introduce a course like Dartmouth's English 2, which would certainly be attractive to most English departments, should first pause to consider whether such a course does indeed serve the best interests of the freshmen who must take it—whether, that is, students are mature enough and have read widely enough by the age of eighteen to profit from a course of this sort. And, as with Dartmouth's English 1, they should consider also whether so indirect an approach to the teaching of writing discharges adequately the English department's responsibility for having accepted a required course in which the teaching of writing is supposed to be the principal concern.

AN ANALYSIS OF THE WRITING OF DARTMOUTH FRESHMEN

An early step in the Dartmouth study was to analyze a sizable cross section of student writing from English 1 and 2. Such an analysis would give a fairly exact notion of how well or poorly Dartmouth freshmen were writing in these two courses, of the ways in which they were writing well or poorly, and of the amount of progress they were making between the beginning and end of each course. Inevitably, the results of the analysis would have some significance for the teaching of writing at other colleges than Dartmouth.

From students enrolled in English 1 and 2 in the fall term 1960, a 20 per cent random sample was taken, which came to 110 students from English 1 and 55 from English 2. The students were selected in such a way that every teacher who had a section of either of these two courses in this term was represented equally. Three papers by each student were secured after they had been marked and graded by the teacher and revised and returned by the student. In English 1, where usually seven themes are written, the second, fourth, and seventh papers were chosen. (It seemed unwise to use the first theme assigned in the course. Since it is written before the student has become acquainted with the standards expected in a college English course, it is often marred by the pretentious writing that many freshmen hopefully think will impress a college professor.) These papers represented the kind of work being done at the beginning, middle, and end of the term and furnished an approximate record of whatever progress the students had made during the term. In English 2, where teachers assign fewer papers, the second and last papers were selected and one from as near the middle of the term as possible. From the two courses there was a total of 495 papers, which amounted roughly to 380,000 words of freshman writing.

The method of analysis used was an obvious one: to classify and record all errors, infelicities, weaknesses, and other negative criticisms that the teachers had noted on the papers. (Only the original version of the papers was considered; revisions by the students were ignored.) In each paper every marked word or passage was closely studied in context to make as sure as possible that the particular error or weakness was being correctly identified. For example, when a teacher had marked something as "awkward" or had placed a question mark beside a word or construction or had rewritten a passage, it was necessary to try to identify the exact difficulty that the teacher had had in mind and to classify it accordingly. A question mark might indicate an inexact choice of word or an error in reasoning or a doubtful interpretation. A passage might have been recast by the teacher to eliminate wordiness or to demonstrate a more effective word order or to achieve greater unity. A certain amount of pure speculation was inevitable in this process. As the analysis proceeded, a detailed system of classification was worked out that included errors and deficiencies of every sort, from those in structure, focus, and "content" to those in the rhetoric of the paragraph, diction, and punctuation.

In spite of several obvious disadvantages, this method of analysis seemed preferable to having two or three readers mark the papers independently. In dealing with such subjective data, it seemed better to rely on the composite judgment of twenty-two competent staff members than on that of any two or three individuals. It is true that those making the analysis sometimes found a word or construction marked as an error that they themselves would have been inclined to let pass without comment, either because it seemed too slight or too debatable, or because they did not agree that it was an error at all—lack of a serial comma before "and," for example, or failure to use a comma after a short adverbial opener, or insistence on the cloudy distinction between "shall" and "will." And sometimes they noticed things that they would have considered errors but that had not been marked—a poorly organized paragraph, perhaps, or a faulty transition. The only errors not marked by the teacher that were included in the tally were occasional misspellings that had obviously been overlooked.

The error list below, though a somewhat simplified version of the one actually used, shows the categories that were set up. These categories, which grew directly out of the criticisms that the English staff had made of the papers, are for the most part reasonably distinct; but inevitably some of them overlap. Under the heading "Words," for example, what is here called "Inflated writing"—pretentious, high-flown, pompous expression—may also be verbosity. Under "Material" a wrong interpretation may arise in part from an error in logic. Under "Sentences" an unclear reference may produce ambiguity, and a stringy sentence may be responsible for a lack of emphasis. And so on. The classification of a particular error often depended on a subjective decision to favor one category over another where clearly more than one choice was possible.

ERROR LIST

A. *Focus and Structure*

1. Unclear, inconsistent, or inappropriate purpose
2. Inconsistent or unclear point of view
3. Inconsistent or inappropriate tone
4. Inadequately limited subject
5. Lack of unity
6. Faulty organization
7. Inadequate or ineffective development
8. Ineffective beginning
9. Ineffective ending

B. *Material*

1. Lack of specificity
2. Insufficient or faulty illustrations or examples
3. Inadequate or inaccurate evidence
4. Redundancy
5. Faulty logic
6. Unwarranted or mistaken assumption
7. Wrong or inadequate interpretation
8. Irrelevance
9. Undue obviousness
10. Mistaken fact(s)

C. *Paragraphs*

1. Lack of unity
2. Ineffective arrangement
3. Inadequate development
4. Lack of consecutiveness
5. Excessive length
6. Unnecessary or inaccurate paragraph division
7. Fused paragraph (failure to divide at logical point)
8. Lack of or faulty transitions between paragraphs

D. *Sentences*

1. Lack of unity
2. Inaccurate parallelism
3. Lack of or inaccurate subordination
4. Excessive subordination

D. *Sentences* (*cont.*)

5. Inexact or ineffective word order
6. Dangling or misplaced modifier
7. Unclear or inexact reference
8. Incomplete construction
9. Shifted or inconsistent construction
10. Inaccurate or incomplete comparison
11. Ambiguous, vague, or obscure meaning
12. Choppy sentences
13. Stringy sentences
14. Unemphatic wording or construction

E. *Words*

1. Inappropriate use of slang
2. Inappropriate use of colloquialism
3. Incorrect idiom
4. Failure to use concrete and specific diction
5. Triteness (including cliché)
6. Inflated writing (including euphemism)
7. Wordiness
8. Jargon
9. Faulty repetition
10. Wrong or inexact word or wording
11. Mixed or inappropriate figure of speech
12. Lack of euphony
13. Omitted word(s)
14. Undesirable coinage

F. *Grammar*

1. Nouns: error in number

2. Nouns: error in case
3. Pronouns: error in case
4. Verbs: error in principal part
5. Verbs: error in tense
6. Verbs: error in mood
7. Incorrect use of adverb or adverbial element
8. Incorrect use of adjective or adjectival element
9. Error in agreement: subject-verb
10. Error in agreement: pronoun-antecedent

G. *Punctuation and Mechanics*

1. Error in use of period
2. Error in use of question mark
3. Error in use of exclamation mark
4. Error in use of colon
5. Error in use of semicolon
6. Error in use of comma
7. Error in use of quotation marks
8. Error in use of dash
9. Error in use of hyphen
10. Error in use of parentheses
11. Error in use of capitals
12. Error in use of abbreviations
13. Error in use of numerals
14. Error in word division
15. Error in use of italics
16. Error in use of apostrophe

H. *Misspelling*

The categories provide a fairly comprehensive system of classifying the weaknesses of a piece of expository writing. The plan is of course negative in its approach, and this circumstance perhaps limits its usefulness. On the other hand, the marks and comments that teachers put on papers are in fact nearly all negative, whether they should be or not. The readers found occasional favorable criticisms in the papers, but they were usually stated in such general terms that it did not seem profitable to record them as part of the data used in the analysis. Besides, if the categories include weaknesses in logic, rhetoric, and "content" ("ideas," "material") as well as more superficial matters, it may be argued that the absence of a defect ought to mean the presence of its corresponding virtue. If, for example, a paper is not marked as defective in point of view or organization or reasoning, one should be able to assume that in the teacher's opinion the point of view has been satisfactorily established and maintained and that the paper is effectively organized and well reasoned. The argument assumes, of course, that the teacher has read the paper attentively and marked it conscientiously, but with respect to the Dartmouth English staff this appears to be a safe assumption. Almost no papers in the nearly 500 that were examined betrayed signs of hasty or careless reading.

To make it easier to total errors of particular kinds, each error type was given a code number; when an error of this type was encountered, its code number was recorded on an IBM "open-face" card along with a code to identify the theme, course, author, and similar data. With the help of IBM machines, this information was punched into the cards and then was analyzed in a number of ways. Some of these proved fruitful; others did not. Though impressive-looking statistical tables were prepared to record the results of each analysis, it was apparent that these tables had to be interpreted with great caution. They looked "scientific" and "objective" enough, but they were after all based on highly subjective data. One of the few categories of error that left no room for subjective interpretation was spelling: Either a word is spelled right or it is not. With nearly all other errors and defects, the question of whether they were in fact errors or defects, and if so of which particular kind, rested on the subjective judgment of individual English teachers. And their judgment in turn often had to be interpreted and thus

GOSHEN COLLEGE LIBRARY
GOSHEN, INDIANA

perhaps modified by the judgment of the three people who classified the errors.

The laborious analysis of 380,000 words of freshman writing in this manner may seem the long way around to a simple objective: to find out how well or poorly a representative sample of freshmen are writing in their freshman English courses. The fact is, however, that the objective is far from simple—indeed, it is extremely complex, unless one is content to approach the problem on a level so general that the answers one gets are almost useless. The method used, in spite of its obvious limitations, did make it possible for the three people doing the analyzing to become thoroughly familiar with a representative cross section of the writing of Dartmouth freshmen and, equally important, with the methods and standards used by the Dartmouth English staff as teachers of composition. These impressions, though subjective, were not therefore the less valuable.

RATE OF ERRORS PER 1,000 WORDS
OF WRITING IN ENGLISH 1 AND 2

TYPE OF ERROR	ENGLISH 1			ENGLISH 2		
	TH. 1	TH. 2	TH. 3	TH. 1	TH. 2	TH. 3
A. Focus and structure	0.76	0.76	0.87	0.52	0.37	0.19
B. Material	3.53	3.24	2.75	2.30	1.87	1.97
C. Paragraphs	1.01	0.68	0.49	0.41	0.58	0.23
D. Sentences	4.84	3.57	2.30	3.27	2.97	2.56
E. Words	10.09	7.26	8.13	6.02	7.12	5.28
F. Grammar	1.17	0.82	0.76	0.56	0.43	0.36
G. Punctuation and mechanics	4.79	3.55	3.37	3.16	4.22	3.47
H. Spelling	3.62	2.59	2.33	2.28	3.01	2.16

Only one of the tables that were prepared will be quoted at this point, though later some of the data of others will be drawn on. The table given above shows the rate of errors in the three themes analyzed in both English 1 and 2. To make the comparison of one theme to another more meaningful, the figures have been adjusted to show the rate of errors not per theme (for individual themes vary in length) but per 1,000 words of writing. That is, the figures given show how many errors of a certain type would be found in a particular theme if all themes were 1,000 words long and all the errors in, say, the first theme in English 1 or the third in English 2 were averaged out. Only the eight general categories of errors have been used in the table because, when the errors are viewed at this level of generalization, the danger of disagreement over how to classify individual errors is relatively slight. That is, though there may be a question whether a specific error should be called one in wordiness or one in jargon, there can be no doubt that it falls under the general head of errors in diction. These eight error types are sufficiently distinct so that it is worthwhile knowing whether any trends appear in their frequency from one theme to the next or between one course and the other.[2]

The following observations can be made about these figures and about the more detailed information on which they are based:

1. One of the first things that strikes the eye in this table is the high rate of errors in diction as compared with the other categories. The obvious explanation is that there are more words in a paper than there are sentences and paragraphs and therefore more possibilities for error. But this is not all of it. Personal preferences of the teacher seem to be reflected more prominently in matters of word choice than elsewhere: of 2,931 diction errors marked in the papers, 981—an even third—were in the category headed "Wrong or inexact word." (Another 726—a fourth of the total—were errors in wordiness.) Also related is the fact that students in their first year of college are rapidly expanding their vocabularies; and as they try to extend their control over more and more words, they are certain to make more mistakes for a time. The student who at the end of English 1 writes in a paper on *Paradise Lost* that Adam and Eve "do not understand why they should be suddenly

[2] In trying to interpret such trends, one must remember that the method of cataloging these errors assumed that, in general, Dartmouth English teachers mark all or nearly all errors that they detect in a paper. A study of the papers indicates that the assumption is a fairly safe one. A few teachers who in some themes appear to be relatively "light" markers actually mark progressively. That is, they consciously refrain from marking every error in early papers, believing that the student should concentrate on a few kinds of mistakes at a time. Sometimes, too, one finds a lightly marked paper that bears a note to the student asking him to schedule a conference with the teacher at which presumably the teacher will criticize the paper in more detail. But such instances are the exception, not the rule.

extricated from Eden" might have said at the beginning of the term that they did not understand why they should be thrown out. The student who writes "we can deduct from this fact" is still not clear about the distinction between *deduct,* which he probably remembers having met in other contexts in high school, and the less familiar *deduce.* This rapid growth of vocabulary in the freshman year may help to explain what appears, from the table, to be only a negligible improvement in diction between the beginning and end of the term in both courses; as students master one word, they encounter other new ones and will misuse some of them until corrected or until further observation teaches them the accepted meaning.

2. In nearly all categories, and in both courses, the table shows that errors decrease between the beginning and end of the term. There is naturally some comfort in this fact, because it means that in the judgment of the staff the quality of the writing improves in most respects during the term—a conclusion borne out also by the higher grades given on the later papers as compared with those written early in the two courses.[3] Unfortunately, there is less comfort here than might be wished, since the rate of errors at the end of the term is seldom a great deal lower than it was at the beginning; and in two instances ("Focus and Structure," English 1, and "Punctuation and Mechanics," English 2) the rate is slightly higher at the end.

3. The table shows relatively few errors in "Focus and Structure" and in "Paragraphs." The obvious explanation is that both of these categories involve larger units of material, of which there are consequently fewer in a given paper than there are sentences; and therefore fewer opportunities for error exist. But another consideration is that errors or shortcomings in these matters are harder to detect and identify than are mistakes in, for example, sentence rhetoric or diction, which are likely to be specific and easily seen. For this reason some teachers do not always mark errors in these two categories, either because they miss them or because, though they sense their presence, they do not take time to

[3] The following table shows the grades given to the first and last themes analyzed from each course:

GRADE	ENGLISH 1		ENGLISH 2	
	FIRST THEME	LAST THEME	FIRST THEME	LAST THEME
A	1	4	4	10
B	15	37	15	20
C	53	53	26	23
D	28	13	8	1
E	13	3	2	0

identify them precisely but content themselves with some general remark at the end of the paper about organization, unity, transitions, coherence, or the like.

Although few of these errors may have been marked in the papers, they are nevertheless likely to be serious because they affect a larger segment of thought than do errors in individual sentences or words. A lack of clear purpose, a muddled pattern of development, a confused paragraph, though reckoned in the table only as single errors, would generally be more serious impediments to clear and effective communication than individual errors in such things as pronoun reference and idiom.

4. Except for spelling and the purely conventional uses of punctuation, none of the categories listed in the table is a simple matter of memorizing rules or forms and then applying them. Instead, they are all closely bound up with the writer's thought and thought processes, and one cannot profitably talk about them without taking account of the thinking that lies behind them. "The first half of your essay," writes one teacher on a D paper, "while interesting, is beside the point. The rest of your essay is too summary, too general. Your first job is to focus on the subject; your second, to deal with it significantly, in depth and in detail." Another teacher writes on a paper to which he has given a D+, "Your first paragraph seems to me scattered. What is the relation between the unconnected first two sentences? The other sentences likewise lack connecting logic." Another writes, "You never do prove your point. You want to prove that Adam is guiltier than Eve, but you spend two-thirds of the paper in talking about Eve and only one-third on Adam. The balance is way off. . . . You still do not get the reader from one idea to the next."

If such errors and shortcomings proceed from mediocre thinking, which in turn proceeds from a mediocre mind, the English teacher can do little; he has no supernatural powers to instill intelligence where it is lacking. But if the errors result from an inefficient approach to the subject or from an ineffective presentation of it, then—assuming that the student wishes to learn—the English teacher is not helpless: He can acquaint the student with the principles of orderly thinking and effective expression (the principles of logic and rhetoric) and provide him with frequent opportunity to practice the application of these principles under expert supervision.

Obviously, the composition teacher cannot by himself, in a few months of class, transform a confused and inept thinker into one whose mind works clearly and logically, any more than he can in the same length of time singlehandedly turn an inept writer into one who writes with fluency and some distinction. But he must nevertheless consider it a principal responsibility to advance that student as far as he can toward these goals. A student who cannot think systematically cannot be expected to write a well-organized paper of any complexity; and if he is to improve his ability to organize ideas, obviously he must learn to think in a more consecutive fashion. All his teachers must bear a hand to help him, each working with the data of his own subject. The composition teacher, by a conscious focus on rhetoric and logic and on disciplined practice in writing, should be able to give the wisest and most effective help.

5. Though it is not apparent from the table, a study of the summary or evaluative comments made on the last papers of the two courses (but especially English 1) reveals that by far the most frequent reasons mentioned by teachers for giving low grades (C−, D, E) to these papers are errors or deficiencies in focus and structure and in material. On the evidence of these comments, the two categories between them account for about eight times more of these low grades than do errors in grammar, punctuation and mechanics, and spelling. Two conclusions are suggested: one, that with the kind of student admitted to Dartmouth, the so-called mechanical errors of writing are rarely fatal after the first few papers of the term; the other, that the more closely a defect in writing is related to fundamental thought processes, the more difficult it is to do anything about it in a few weeks. The kind of sustained intellectual discipline that is called for must be a responsibility of the entire faculty, not just the English department; and since thought is rarely precise until it has found overt expression in symbols, the best way for the faculty to enforce this discipline would be to require as much careful writing as possible and to judge it rigorously for cogency and clarity.

6. As one might expect in a college as highly selective in its admission policy as Dartmouth, students in the freshman English courses make fewer gross errors in the mechanical aspects of writing than do most students at less selective colleges. This is not to say that all Dartmouth freshmen write well; though a few of them do, a great many write with surprising ineptness. But their shortcomings involve mechanics less often than they do those matters of logic, rhetoric, and content whose cure is much slower and more difficult. It is surprising to discover how slight a problem certain mechanical errors are in freshman English at Dartmouth, errors that at some other colleges and universities may almost monopolize the English teacher's time. For example, in the nearly 500 papers and 380,000 words of freshman writing that were analyzed, there were exactly 5 fused ("run-together") sentences, 35 sentence fragments, and 20 comma splices (6 of them concentrated in a single paper). In all this

writing there were only 85 errors in apostrophes (both in possessives and in contractions), only 40 errors in subject-verb agreement, only 20 in pronoun-antecedent agreement. To someone who has taught remedial composition in less selective institutions, such a state of affairs seems almost utopian.[4]

7. The unreasonableness of English spelling is a handicap that all literate users of English suffer from, whether bright or dull, whether students at Dartmouth College or at Elkhorn Community College. Dartmouth freshmen misspell more words than they should, but still relatively few when compared with the average at most other colleges. In the 380,000 words of writing from English 1 and 2, there were only 851 misspellings, excluding errors in apostrophes and those clearly due to carelessness ("teh" for "the," "obligind" for "obliging"). With the careless errors figured in, the total was still only 1,064, an average of 1 misspelling for every 357 words. Even this figure seems worse than it is, for many of the errors were concentrated in the work of relatively few students. The state of spelling in the freshman class at Dartmouth is still considerably short of perfection, to be sure, but it is not a situation about which a teacher would feel such black despair as he would if he were teaching at a college where a single two-page paper in a remedial class may contain 30 or 40 misspellings.[5]

[4] See Appendix C for a typical failing theme from Dartmouth's English 1 and one from a remedial course at a state university.

[5] Here is a fair specimen of the type:

Best Pets

Dogs, are said to be mans best friend. Whether this statement is true or not is a matter of opnnion, and dose not have a great bearing on this story. However it is commonly considered that the male sex pefer dogs and the female sex pefer cats as there favoret pets. This is not altogether true, for there are in my estimation two typs of small animle lovers the kinds that like cats, and the kind that hate cats, witch consist of both sexes.

Some people are afflicted of the desease known as cat fobia, when they see a cat they get chills and often pass out. Still others (for example James Mason) love cats with a passion and keep great numbers aeround their houses. Whether dogs or cats are the best pets is very debateable, each has his own however being one of those who come under the cat lover class I am incline to choos cats. Cats however can not be trained to do usful things as dogs can, and are seldom use for outstanding profession as watching houses or carrying brandy. But for pets they are very fine animels, they do not bark or chew on rugs.

The significance of this analysis lies mainly in what it reveals about the nature of the writing difficulties that this kind of student —at Dartmouth and probably elsewhere as well—exhibits when he is writing for a highly critical reader and therefore is trying to write as well as he possibly can. He does not make many gross errors in grammar or usage, nor is he what could be called a really bad speller. But he makes other and more serious mistakes. During his freshman English course he progresses visibly in reducing the frequency of most kinds of errors in his writing even when no class time is devoted to a study of these matters. The disciplined practice in writing required by these courses appears to have the favorable effect that one would expect it to have. But although the number of errors being made by the end of the term is usually lower than at the beginning, it is seldom enough lower to be a cause for genuine satisfaction. Errors in the larger aspects of composition persist— especially those that fall under what has here been called "Focus and Structure" and "Material"—and teachers rightly view these as serious defects. Unfortunately, errors of this sort are not easily eliminated, for they are inseparable from the thought that the student is trying to express. The only remedy is for the student to learn to think more clearly and to continue to stock his mind—obviously not responsibilities that are the concern of teachers of only one department.

Teachers of freshman English, even when they are blessed with superior students like these, have a responsibility to exert a steady pressure on their students to eliminate errors in spelling and gross errors in grammar and usage and to reduce less serious errors to a minimum. The great majority of students at reputable colleges have the capacity to master these conventions if they know that they must; but unfortunately, as a rule it is only the English teacher who can be counted on to take the time and trouble to hold students to the high standard that is necessary.

The often negligible decline in number of errors between the first and last of the term that the analysis reveals suggests that the English teacher ought to try whenever possible to identify for the student the principles of clear thought and effective expression that animate good expository prose, so that when the student violates one of these principles, he will be able to do more than correct the one particular error, then make the same error again in another context. Instead, if he is made aware of the principle behind the error, he should eventually be able to generalize from the principle and avoid most errors of this class in the future. Such instruction ought to benefit the great majority of college freshmen, not just the bright ones. The analysis also underlines the importance of maintaining a continuing pressure on the student to think through what he wants to say, then express it in language faithful to the thought (that is, accurate) and considerate of the reader (that is, effective and correct). A responsibility so complex, one so inseparable from the student's general intellectual development, cannot be effectively discharged by a single teacher in a single class. Rather, it must be accepted by all the student's teachers through all four years of his undergraduate education.

HOW COMPOSITION IS TAUGHT AT DARTMOUTH

Although a main reason for studying so closely a large number of themes by Dartmouth freshmen was to provide the kind of information presented in the last section, another was to learn in as much detail as possible how the English department at a first-class college assigns and marks compositions, for these activities are central in teaching writing. The problems that were found to arise were, not surprisingly, much the same ones that arise wherever freshman English is taught. The explanation probably is that since most college English teachers are not explicitly trained to teach composition (as they *are* trained to teach literature), they use a great many rule-of-thumb procedures when they teach writing; and these procedures tend to generate the same problems wherever they are used.

Most of the shortcomings that one can point to in the way papers are assigned and marked in the Dartmouth freshman English courses can be traced to what seems to be too wide a variation in practice or in standards from one teacher to another. This is not to suggest that variation itself is undesirable; on the contrary, a certain amount of variation is not only inevitable but wholesome, a sign of vigor and conviction. The question, rather, is how much variation should exist, especially in a required course offered in many sections. If there is not considerable uniformity in all sections, the students who must take the course cannot be sure of getting the training or the knowledge that the course is supposed to give as a condition of its being required. Where the line is to be drawn between liberty and license in these matters is the business of a department to decide for itself. Certainly a majority should not ride roughshod over the convictions of colleagues who have other views; nor, on the other hand, should a recalcitrant minority consider themselves infallible and everyone else confounded in error.[6] A broad middle ground can be defined that will neither hamper individuality nor permit it to get out of hand.

The first respect in which too much variation seems to exist is in the care with which writing assignments are made. In a course in composition, a teacher can scarcely give too much attention to this matter, for the success of his students is to some extent in proportion to his success in framing a good assignment for them to work at. Nearly half a century ago Rollo Walter Brown, though writing about composition in school rather than in college, spoke to English teachers in terms that are still relevant:

> We are strangely illogical. If we do even the smallest piece of writing ourselves, we think upon it, and only after we have digested it thoroughly do we venture to write. Nevertheless, when we assign a theme, which, to begin with, is looked upon by the pupil as a mere task set by some one else, we frequently do not discuss the material in any thoroughgoing manner, and we do not always show the pupil how he might become interested in his subject by talking to his classmates and friends about it. We do not help him far in getting ideas, save in a very general way, and we hesitate to put a plan on the blackboard, lest he copy it and use it. We give him only the lightest straw to clutch—sometimes only a title of four or five words—yet expect him to come out safely, and to find pleasure in the struggle. He probably does neither. His mind is unaccustomed to catching up stray ideas and putting them in order. He may not even do his best in trying to learn how. He writes what little is in his mind, or fits together some ideas that he has garbled from a book, and calls the result his "composition." Then we spend many precious minutes showing him, or trying to show him, how to tear his ideas all apart and rewrite them into a new

[6] Required reading for all college English teachers, but especially those who fear that administrative paternalism is inhibiting the teacher's freedom in the classroom, is Robert B. Heilman's lively article "The Cult of Personality: Hell's Spells," *College English*, 23:91–98, 1961.

theme. Certainly there is little pedagogical or personal defense for our practice. If the teacher helps his pupils to enrich, quicken, and organize their material before they begin to write, he not only stimulates them to their best efforts, but saves himself infinite pains.[7]

The study of almost 500 marked and graded English papers at Dartmouth revealed that the fault of which Brown complained may still appear, even in a strong English department at a first-rate college. Some teachers give writing assignments that are too open-ended, that lack point and direction, that leave students too much on their own for the experience of composing a paper to have as much value as it might. For example, five papers selected at random from those written for a single assignment in one class bore the following titles: "The Oasis" (a discourse on eating dinner at a college dining hall), "Intellectual Curiosity," "Character Analysis of Cassius" (in *Julius Caesar*), "The Mt. Washington Cog Railway," and "The Rise and Fall of Communism." It is hard to avoid the conclusion that this teacher simply told his class to go home and write a theme. Significantly, both the theme on "Intellectual Curiosity" and that on "The Rise and Fall of Communism" were marked down by the teacher for dealing with excessively broad subjects in too limited an amount of space.

The analysis showed that sometimes, even when the assignment is expressly restricted to the literature being read, the topic may be only "Assess the role of Enobarbus" or "Discuss the conflict between love and patriotism in *Antony and Cleopatra*" or even "Write a paper in which you give your impressions of *Richard III*." As topics for papers in a literature course, these may be unexceptionable. As topics for papers in a composition course, they are less than satisfactory. The distinction is that between testing and teaching. If, for example, a literature-centered course in freshman English is to be viewed primarily as a course in literature, then the themes become a kind of open-book examination and the teacher is understandably reluctant to help the student beforehand to compose his answers except in so far as class discussion may help him to do so. But if such a course is considered to be mainly one in composition, then the teacher should plan the writing assignments with this end in

[7] *How the French Boy Learns to Write: A Study in the Teaching of the Mother Tongue*, Cambridge, Mass.: Harvard University Press, 1915, pp. 222–223.

view. If a word of caution ahead of time from the teacher will prevent most of the students, or even a handful of them, from making useless mistakes that the teacher must only try to explain later after they have been made, he is well advised to take the trouble to explain them in the first place. Thus if a teacher decides to assign his class to write on cynicism in *Richard III*, he should expect that a considerable part of the class will need to be reminded that it is important to define terms at the outset. If he does not remind them when he makes the assignment, he will later find himself writing on paper after paper, "You should have established at the beginning an authoritative definition of *cynicism, cynical,* and *cynic.*"

But some teachers give a great deal of care to planning assignments for papers, trying to anticipate the special problems posed by a topic and pointing these out to their students so that they will learn systematically, and presumably do the best work they are capable of. The following is an example of this kind of assignment given by a Dartmouth teacher. It was duplicated and handed out to his students.

THEME ASSIGNMENT NUMBER THREE

The triumph of God's "ministers of chastisement" at the end of *Richard III* would seem to dramatize the triumph of good over evil and the reestablishment of the moral order in place of civil strife. Does the victory of the triumvirate in *Julius Caesar* augur as well for the future of Rome?

Some general observations:
1. You must ask yourself questions about the kinds of evidence available to you in solving this problem. Do not argue from what you know or may learn about Roman history after the fall and death of Caesar. *Look for your evidence inside the play.* The following questions may help you formulate a conclusion:
   a. How does the tone of the closing scene of *Julius Caesar* compare with the tone of the closing scene of *Richard III*?
   b. What do you know from the play about the characters of the men who now rule Rome?
   c. Is the fact that Rome is now ruled by three men rather than by one of any significance?
   These are obviously only sample questions; you can think of dozens more.

2. The chief difficulty which you will want to overcome in this paper, I should think, will be the marshalling and organization of evidence in support of your thesis. You are going to have to write about the characters of Octavius, Antony, and Lepidus, for example. How are you going to keep this theme from splitting up into several papers?

The teaching of freshman English varies also because teachers require different types of writing. In the sort of literature-centered course being discussed here, there is usually a general understanding that themes will be based on the various literary works that are studied, the theory being that both the instruction in literature and that in writing will be made more effective by this interrelationship. But some teachers apparently feel hampered by such a restriction and often ask for compositions of a different sort. In English 1 at Dartmouth, for example, probably close to a fourth of all themes written in a given term are on nonliterary subjects and take a great variety of forms. These may include autobiographical papers ("My First Job"), personal narratives ("The Final Race," an account of a boat race), descriptive sketches ("A Hanover Walk in Mid-October"), character sketches ("One in a Million," a favorite high school teacher), personal essays on familiar subjects ("Casting for Fresh Water Bass"), informative essays ("The Connecticut Valley Tobacco Industry"), "opinion" essays ("What Worship Service Means to Me"), short-short stories ("Ten Thousand Suns," a fantasy about the bombing of Hiroshima), book reviews ("Maxim Gorky's *The Lower Depths*"), dramatic skits (an assignment involving Hitler and Mussolini as parallels to characters in *Julius Caesar*), and letters to editors, congressmen, government agencies, business firms. Some of these papers are at least as well written as the more usual critical papers on literary works. Others, such as the dramatic skits on Mussolini and Hitler (which were required of an entire class), can range from the inept to the disastrous—in this instance not surprising, in view of most students' total inexperience with writing in dramatic form and their nebulous knowledge of Hitler and Mussolini.

Most of the papers in this group are likely to be based on personal experience and on personal opinion of nonliterary matters. Papers of this sort have undoubted attractions, else so many teachers —and not just at Dartmouth—would not assign them. They are, for one thing, easier in some ways for students to write. The subject matter is likely to be close to the students: They will have plenty to say and will usually be interested in saying it. They will approach these subjects with less self-consciousness than they will subjects more remote from their immediate experience and so will often write better, particularly at the beginning of the course when for many students writing is still an unaccustomed exercise that half-paralyzes them. Papers on subjects like "A Hanover Walk in Mid-October" can provide excellent training in observation, and those on such subjects as "College and the Agnostic" can offer training in distinguishing between fact and opinion, in supporting generalizations, and in reasoning clearly—as of course can the critical papers on literary works also. Above all, an occasional paper of this sort can provide a welcome change of pace for both student and teacher. Even the best student in a literature-based course may long once in a while for a chance to write on something besides Shakespeare. Even the most devoted teacher of Milton may find that his appreciation has become jaded after he has read the twentieth—or the fortieth—paper on the temptation of Eve.

It seems doubtful that anyone would want to rule out this kind of paper as an occasional exercise, regardless of the content and aims of the freshman course. But in a course that asks students to read standard literature and expects them to master the techniques of writing exposition, the number of such papers ought to be limited rather carefully. Papers that report personal experience provide a kind of training in composition that, while certainly not without value, is clearly of a different sort from that provided by papers of analysis and criticism. Personal opinion papers on nonliterary subjects offer the proper training in expository writing, but they deprive the student of the considerable advantage of relating what he writes to what he reads.

The remaining variations that will be mentioned concern not the assignment of papers but the marking and grading of them. The first is a wide range in the intensiveness with which papers are marked—noticeable at Dartmouth but certainly not peculiar to it. Probably most English teachers, if they have time to read their papers with care, are inclined to overmark. A misused semicolon or an off-center idiom afflicts them like an uncontrollable itch, and they are not comfortable again until they have scarified the error with a red pencil. What this sometimes means is that early papers in the freshman course may come back to their authors with as many as seventy or seventy-five errors marked in three pages or less of prose. There may be nothing wrong with this practice. Certainly the student has been given a powerful demonstration of the full extent of his shortcomings, and the teacher rests secure in the knowledge that he has done his duty. But it seems doubtful whether a student who makes this many mistakes has the ability to concentrate effectively on eliminating so many all at once. He is more likely to be stunned instead. Probably this question, like many others in the pedagogy of composition, cannot be settled in any final sense. But marking this many errors is so time-consuming and laborious that teachers who follow the practice might find it profitable sometimes to try another method that also has its supporters: to mark selectively, concentrating on certain types of errors at first and leaving others unmarked, then moving in later papers to other kinds as the first begin to diminish. Those who defend this method testify that many of the kinds of errors that have gone unmarked in the early papers vanish from later papers without help from the teacher as students get more in the habit of writing up to a standard. This is particularly true of minor errors in mechanics and of slips in proofreading.

At the other extreme, some teachers undermark their papers, placing three or four marks in the margin, a gnomic comment at the end, and a C— at the top. If this sparse marking is supplemented later by a private conference with the student, at which the paper is gone over closely, few would want to find fault with the practice. But if these half-dozen marks and the grade are all the student has to guide him on the path to improvement, he may find the going difficult. A reasonable middle ground between the two extremes should be possible.

Another fertile source of variation is the teachers' judgment of what constitutes an error. To be sure, no reasonable person can expect complete agreement on this score, except on a relatively small list of matters, of which spelling is the most obvious. Most aspects of grammar may be included too, though with less certainty: In most contexts only purists would object to the plural verb in "a large number of passengers were killed in the crash"—but there are purists aplenty in the ranks of English teachers, and as a rule

they are extraordinarily vocal. Questions of effective paragraph
structure, of sentence variety, of word order, of choice of language
are much more difficult to agree on, because judgment of them
depends on one's sense of their fitness not only in themselves but
also in relation to other aspects of the composition. It is even more
difficult to judge the effectiveness of a line of argument; of the
student's choice of a particular pattern of organization; of proportion, unity, development, and the many other important though
elusive qualities that must be considered in evaluating a piece of
writing.

Even when all this is taken into account, English teachers—at
Dartmouth and elsewhere—should still try to agree as closely as they
can. It should not be hard to settle some matters. For example,
teachers of composition obviously should be familiar with a system
of English grammar and its basic terminology—whether "old" or
"new" grammar is not especially important for this limited purpose, which is simply to know what is going on in a sentence and to
agree on names to call things by. It is a notable irony that in the
present state of affairs neither undergraduate nor graduate training
in English can be guaranteed to provide this knowledge: As a
freshman the future English teacher is usually exempted from composition and grammar study and put in a literature course; as an
English major he is, more often than not, permitted to graduate
without a course in the history of the English language or in English grammar or in linguistics;[8] as a graduate student he will probably take Chaucer and Old English but still may avoid a course in
the grammar of modern English. This curious situation may explain
why highly educated English teachers sometimes write on a student
theme such comments as "You have a dangling participle here; get
rid of it," when in fact no participle is in sight; or why they mark
a student down for writing "We drove slow for the next several
miles," unaware that both *slow* and *slowly* have been in good use as
adverbs for centuries. The remedy is simple: a little homework for
the teachers.

---

[8] Or in rhetorical theory or advanced expository composition or logic—in
most of the subjects, in fact, that would help to prepare him to teach composition with the same expertness that he brings to the teaching of literature.
See Appendix B for a suggested minimum list of books that a teacher of
composition in college should be familiar with.

The problem of agreeing on standards of usage is more difficult, since usage (as English teachers know, and other people seem often not to know) is not immutable but in a constant state of change. Today's good usage is sometimes the slang of yesterday (*mob, cab, piano*). Yesterday's good usage may sound affected today ("if it be she") or be ungrammatical ("the most unkindest cut of all," or Hamlet's question to Polonius, "Between who?").

More than that, though it is generally accepted that a course in composition should require students to use the standard English of educated people, educated people do not speak and write in a single uniform way. Within the bounds of "good English" there can still be wide variation. E. B. White's "Once More to the Lake," though undoubtedly written in "good English," is not in the same kind of good English that one sees in Bertrand Russell's "A Free Man's Worship." The difference is in part one of personality— *"le style est de l'homme même"*—but it also reflects differences in purpose, subject, situation, and anticipated readers. This is simply to say that it is dubious practice to forbid students *ever* to use a contraction in writing (to pick a common example), without taking into account whether the writing is of a kind that makes the use of contractions inappropriate. Personal-experience papers may often be enhanced by a judicious use of such marks of an informal and personal tone and might be made stilted by an overscrupulous avoidance of them. Critical papers based on literature are generally —though not always—more formal, because of differences in subject matter and purpose. A teacher may feel that under these circumstances contractions are not appropriate and mark them wrong when he finds them. The important thing is to allow for a reasonable amount of flexibility. While students should by no means be given to understand that "anything goes" and they are their own lawgivers, they should be taught to recognize that good English is appropriate English; that if they wish to be regarded as educated people, they must use the language of educated people; and that educated people do not always speak and write an unvarying formal —or informal—kind of English but adapt their discourse, as they do their behavior in other respects, to the relevant circumstances. It is good pedagogy to assume that college students are fundamentally rational and may be trusted to do likewise.

Accuracy or appropriateness of word choice is another highly individual matter about which English teachers, including those at Dartmouth, are prone to disagree. Anyone who examined several dozen marked papers from Dartmouth's English 1 and 2 or from any other freshman composition course would be struck by the high proportion of errors in wording that have been marked—but also by the degree to which personal preferences, and even idiosyncrasy, have sometimes governed the marking. When a student writes "the scenery in the movie of *Richard III* is quite moderate," the teacher is justified in asking him to substitute the more accurate word *simple* for *moderate* in this context. He can properly suggest to the student who writes "outdoor scenes can be portrayed in their real manner" to write instead the more economical and accurate "portrayed realistically." But when he suggests that "the second contributing factor" be changed to "the second contributing component," he has not helped things very much. Since many people of good taste are offended by the careless overuse of *factor*, the student might properly be asked to find a more exact word here; but *component* is as close to jargon as *factor*, and the alliteration and galloping rhythm of "second contributing component" will strike many ears as more offensive than the original wording. To take another example, it is hard to see what has been gained by making a student change "requires the passengers to assume uncomfortable positions" to "requires that the passengers assume uncomfortable positions." Both constructions are correct, both are idiomatic English. The difference seems to be only that if the teacher had been writing the sentence he would have preferred the clause with its formal subjunctive verb to the infinitive phrase. Some teachers are judicious in their marking of such matters of wording; others should be more careful to make sure that a given phrase or word really offends against good use; and if it does, to make certain that the alternative wording suggested is a genuine improvement.

Teachers sometimes differ considerably in the amount of attention they give to errors in the larger aspects of composition—paragraph structure, over-all organization, purpose, tone, consecutiveness, and similar matters. To be sure, these are the most difficult things to mark in a paper; unlike errors in spelling, idiom, word choice, and the like, they do not always immediately strike the eye but are more likely to be sensed rather than clearly seen at first reading; the teacher must then read through the paper again to identify the trouble exactly. To do so is of course time-consuming, and teachers may often find themselves pressed for time even under the nearly optimum conditions of class size and teaching load that prevail in the Dartmouth English department. Some teachers, however, rarely mark deficiencies in these larger aspects, contenting themselves instead with a grade and a brief note that indicate their dissatisfaction with the paper. Consider, for example, the following paragraph:

> The entire color scheme which Oroszco uses is without a doubt beautiful as well as symbolic. The sky is of a dark reddish hue and the whole picture is bleak in color except for the bright yellow coloring of Christ's body.

This can hardly be said to be a well-developed paragraph, but the only suggestion that was offered for its improvement is that "without a doubt" be deleted. From the C— given the paper, the student will understand that something is wrong; but even though a note at the end admonishes him to "improve your paragraphing" and "practice achieving greater unity," he would have a better chance of doing both if the criticism were more specific. The same is true of a student who is told at the end of his paper that "organization is rather monotonous" or "paper is unfocused." Both criticisms may be warranted, and they are better than no criticisms at all of these defects; but it seems probable that the student would be more likely to avoid similar mistakes in future papers if the ones he has already made are more clearly identified for him.

Teachers should, in fact, take stock from time to time to be sure that the marks and comments they put on papers are of a kind most likely to prove helpful to the student and lead him toward the goal in view: better writing in future papers. As mentioned before, whenever possible the emphasis should be on familiarizing the student with the principle involved, so that he will not only correct the error before him but will be able, by generalizing from the principle, to avoid making the same kind of error again.

Several common practices in paper marking, found probably at all colleges, may be questioned on this score. For example, a teacher confronted by an off-center construction that offends his sense of fitness may, after pondering it a moment, abandon the effort to identify exactly what is wrong and instead circle the passage and merely write "awkward" (or *awk* or *K*) in the margin. Or he may simply circle it and put a question mark or exclamation mark beside it. No doubt sometimes this kind of marking is adequate for the purpose. It would be an obtuse student who required more than a question mark to tell him that something has gone wrong with such a sentence as, "His addition of Jane Shore was as well as being helpful in placing her in time it was definitely admusing"—and it would be a teacher of extraordinary dedication who would feel obliged to unravel all the strands of error here. Usually, though, the teacher is wise to identify the trouble exactly. In "neither of the views of Shaw nor Tillyard would be adequate," the student would be better served if he were told that the error is one in parallelism, rather than being informed simply that the passage is "awkward."

Another frequently used device tending in the same direction is that of rewriting faulty passages for the student instead of identifying the trouble and asking the student to do his own revising. No doubt it is occasionally necessary for the teacher to recast a sentence in his own words as the only practical way, short of a conference with the student, to indicate all the things that ail it. Consider these two sentences: "A second instance of Milton having both a literal and a metaphorical meaning occurs in the description of Hell. The description occurs after the fallen angels have a conference to decide what their retaliations to being forced out of Heaven should be." The teacher, instead of spelling out laboriously everything wrong with this passage, simply rewrote it: "A second instance of Milton's combining both a literal and metaphorical meaning occurs in the description of Hell, after the fallen angels have had a conference to decide how they should retaliate for having been forced out of Heaven." On the other hand, the weaknesses of the following sentence can be easily diagnosed: "Milton's ideas of order in the Universe and the various levels of hierarchy are constantly recurring." The teacher recast it: "Milton's ideas of order and hierarchy in the Universe constantly recur." If he had marked the offending parts of the sentence with the symbols or abbreviations for wordiness and faulty word order, the student ought to have been able to correct the sentence by himself and should have benefited from doing so. This opinion must be advanced with diffidence, however, for some students must be shown as well as told what is wrong. Wordiness in particular seems hard for many students to detect in their own writing, even when the passage has been underlined and labeled for them. The reason probably is that their thought is to them inseparable from the particular pattern in which it emerged on paper, and they find it difficult to tamper with the wording without feeling that at the same time they are somehow violating the thought. Surgery by the teacher is often the only way to convince such students that a passage is not all bone and sinew but is encumbered with a good deal of fat.

Except for a personal conference, the most effective way to show the student where a paper needs improvement and where it is satisfactory is to write comments on the theme. A student whose paper comes back to him marked only with rule numbers and cryptic abbreviations like *coh, ts, X, Z,* and *ab* sometimes feels as though the paper might as well have been run through a machine. He is grateful for any sign that the paper in which he has offered his own interpretations, attitudes, convictions has been read by the teacher with some evidence of personal interest in him as a human being. Although it is possible to bury a student paper under a heap of criticism, as Thomas Wolfe is reported to have done when he taught freshman English at New York University, teachers seldom go to this extreme. Some members of the Dartmouth English staff will occasionally jot numerous comments in the margins, add a note or two on the backs of pages, and conclude with a general evaluation up to half a page long. There is some danger that this much criticism will bewilder the student rather than enlighten him, but it seems better to take the risk than to give him too little criticism, as in a paper marked only with symbols and abbreviations referring to various errors and bearing the single comment "You misspell 'Shakespeare'—for shame!"

The advantages of comments over symbols and abbreviations, other than the evidence they give of the teacher's personal interest, are principally that they can be highly specific, referring not just to a type of error but to a particular error in a particular context, and that they can be used not only to point out errors and weaknesses but to commend the student for a well-turned phrase, a clear line of reasoning, an improvement in sentence structure over previous papers. "I suggest that you use a passive construction in this sentence," writes one Dartmouth teacher in a marginal comment, "to avoid beginning still another sentence with 'I.'" This sort of advice seems much more likely to *teach* the student than would *awk* or *E* (for faulty emphasis) or *R* (for faulty repetition) or *Vc* (wrong voice) or any of the other marks that might be used to indicate that something is wrong with the construction. Another teacher writes, beside a well-written complex sentence, "I am glad to see that you are learning to use subordination effectively." Rule numbers, error symbols, the usual abbreviations, all are useless when the teacher wants to tell a student what he has done well, for all of them are negative. Unfortunately, not enough teachers habitually write comments of this sort in the margins as they mark a paper. Yet it seems fully as important for the student's improvement that he know what he is doing right as that he be told what he is doing wrong.

Many Dartmouth teachers try to include some favorable remarks in the general evaluative comment that they usually put at the end of a paper. At their best, these comments are effective teaching devices:

> This is certainly much better than your last paper. You bring out Enobarbus's shrewd view of things clearly. That Enobarbus commits suicide, however, suggests that your conclusion is rather shaky. Logic cannot govern all relationships and actions, as Enobarbus finds out when he deserts Antony. But perhaps it is a question of what "adjustment" means.
>
> The two major stylistic weaknesses of the paper are wordiness and colloquial phrasing; you must work to eliminate them. The improvement in punctuation is gratifying, though you must watch the "comma splice." Read Section 12C of the *Handbook*.

Perfunctory comments probably do little good: "A thoughtful job, though several points could do with further clarification," or "Organization good, execution loose and awkward," or simply "Good job."

Errors in spelling present a special problem. English teachers everywhere unfailingly mark them, but there is wide disagreement over how seriously to regard such errors—how much, that is, spelling errors should affect the grade given a paper, and eventually the grade given a student at the end of the course.

No informed person tries to defend English spelling on grounds of logic or efficiency or esthetics; it is a monument to bigotry and prejudice, a burden under which every literate user of the language must labor. In spite of the popular view, it is not synonymous with education, nor does mastery of it have any appreciable correlation with intelligence. It is perhaps the only aspect of writing where originality is discouraged, experiment not tolerated. One hundred per cent conformity is demanded.

It is proper to recognize how absurd such a state of affairs is, how opposed to common sense and logic and sound educational practice. It is proper for the teacher to point all this out to the student—indeed, it is only honesty to do so. But the teacher must also emphasize the enormous social importance of conventional spelling. Like it or not, every educated person is expected to spell words in the usual ways. If he does not, the seriousness of the consequences is out of all reasonable proportion to the seriousness of the offense. If a student somehow has failed to grasp this reality before coming to college, it must be brought home to him at the earliest opportunity in his freshman year by all his teachers (not just his English teacher), and with an emphasis that he will not forget. Every college teacher should regard errors in spelling—as indeed any gross errors in grammar and usage—as serious breaches of etiquette, not to be borne in the writing of cultivated people. Avoidance of such blunders should not be considered a virtue for which the student is to be commended, any more than he would be praised for not wiping his hands on the tablecloth or polishing his shoes with the guest towels. It is a minimum standard, to be met without question or remark.

Clearly, then, teachers should be severe in judging papers that are marred by errors in spelling; such errors should drastically affect the grade given the paper. There can be little excuse for a student who misspells words in a paper that he has written outside of class: As one teacher has said, all that is needed for perfect spelling in these circumstances is a dictionary and a thumb. Some students will have to work harder at the job than others will, but anyone who has enough intelligence and seriousness of purpose to justify his presence in a respectable college or university can learn to spell acceptably in all his written work except perhaps that done under extreme pressure, such as examinations; and even in these he can approach much closer to an acceptable standard of spelling than he may think possible—if he is made to try. Much of the bad spelling that college students perpetrate is a result of the permissiveness of their earlier teachers. It is no favor to let them continue on the same path, perhaps reprimanding them orally or in a note on their papers but not lowering their grades.

Though all teachers should insist on good spelling, the English teacher in particular should be severe about spelling errors. One Dartmouth English teacher writes at the end of a paper that he has failed, "You have some interesting things to say about the movie [*Richard III*], but unfortunately I cannot pass a three-page theme that contains seven spelling mistakes." Another teacher, however, may pass a theme of the same length with a D or a C— even though it contains ten or a dozen misspellings. One teacher scolds a student in a note on a short paper: "I should have been more impressed by this if more care had gone into it. Such sloppy writing inevitably suggests careless and superficial thinking." Yet this paper happened to be the last one of the term; it contained ten separate misspellings, and it was given a passing grade. If the English department of a college wavers in its attitude toward errors in spelling, the rest of the faculty, whose cooperation is essential in enforcing a standard for spelling, may be excused for similar laxness. As the saying goes, "If gold rust, what shall iron do?"

One more kind of variation in the marking of English papers remains to be mentioned. It is the most obvious of all: variation in assigning grades. Though no one really expects one teacher's C— to be every other teacher's C—, English departments usually exhibit a variety of standards and a consequent range of grades that have done little to bolster general confidence in English teachers as expert judges of writing.[9] Anyone who has been in the profession

---

[9] Perhaps the most illuminating study of the problem of variation in judging the quality of student compositions is one recently made by Paul B. Diederich, John W. French, and Sydell T. Carlton and reported in a research bulletin of the Educational Testing Service: *Factors in Judgments of Writing Ability*, Princeton, N.J., 1961. With the support of a grant from the Carnegie Corporation, Diederich and his colleagues selected 300 papers written by a representative sample of liberal arts freshmen at Middlebury College, the University of Pennsylvania, and Cornell University. These papers were reproduced exactly, and sets of them were given to fifty-three judges who included college English teachers, social and natural scientists, lawyers, writers and editors, and business executives, all of whom were known to have a keen interest in student writing. Each reader was asked to sort the 300 papers into nine piles arranged in the order of quality and to write the number of the pile on each paper. He

for half a dozen years and taught at two or three colleges will have seen some astonishing displays of idiosyncrasy when several themes are graded and discussed at a staff meeting. It is not unusual to find that one paper is judged all the way from A to E. Ordinarily in such meetings a comfortable majority of the grades given a particular theme will be within a notch of each other—that is, a majority of B's and C's, or of C's and D's. But a few extremists will be out on the edges and will defend their judgment with all the passion and eloquence that a consciousness of virtue can bestow. Aware of these differences among their teachers, students have an ancient pastime of turning the same paper in to two different English instructors, then chortling cynically when one gives it a B and the other a D.

To judge from the evidence of 500 English 1 and 2 papers, the Dartmouth staff agrees about as closely on the quality of student papers as one could reasonably expect—which, to be sure, is not quite the same thing as what one would like. The extent of disagree-

---

was also asked to write a brief comment on each paper saying what he liked or disliked about it.

Ninety-four per cent of the 300 papers received seven, eight, or all nine of the nine possible grades; none of the papers received fewer than five different grades. The correlation of agreement among the fifty-three readers was only .31, and that among the English teachers (who agreed with each other more closely than any of the other groups) was only .41.

Statistical analysis of the comments on the papers revealed that the readers tended to emphasize one or another of five general aspects of the papers: "Ideas," "Form," "Flavor" ("style, interest, sincerity"), "Mechanics," "Wording." Among the interesting conclusions suggested by the analysis was that scores on College Board tests made by the 300 students who had written the papers were unrelated to "Ideas" (correlation of −.02) and almost entirely unrelated to "Form" (correlation of .16) and "Flavor" (correlation of .07). On the other hand, the test scores were significantly related to "Mechanics" and "Wording" (correlations of .50 and .45, respectively).

What this appears to suggest, as John W. French says in a paper based on the study, is that perhaps English teachers have been right all along when they have insisted that a written composition tests things about writing skill that objective tests such as those of the College Board cannot get at. Unfortunately, the wide disagreement among the readers that was revealed by the analysis suggests that the readers (including the English teachers) do not do very well in identifying these qualities either. (French's article, "Schools of Thought in Judging Excellence of English Themes," appeared in the *Proceedings of the Invitational Conference on Testing Problems*, Princeton, N.J., 1961, pp. 19–28.)

ment is much smaller than it would be with a less experienced and less expert staff—the usual aggregation of graduate students and junior instructors, for example, that customarily teaches the freshman course in state universities. But there is enough disagreement to cause some uneasiness and to emphasize the importance of taking steps to keep even an expert staff together on standards for judging student prose. The range illustrated in the grading of the following two papers on *Paradise Lost* from English 1 is not uncommon. Both papers were graded C+, though it is probably safe to predict that most English teachers would find the first paper considerably inferior to the second. A few paragraphs from each will be enough to give an idea of the texture of the prose and the quality of the thinking.

The Punishment of Adam and Eve

It appears from the reading of Genesis, that God's prime purpose in creating the world was his cultivation of life, particularly that of mankind. He engaged in this long, tiresome enterprise simply to foster the "children" of the earth, for whom he could present everlasting life. He focused His attentions on these prime products of His endeavor and was most proud.

For these reasons one can obviously understand His anger at their sudden refusal to obey His divine decree. Adam and Eve had found themselves in a perfectly marvellous situation; they were plunged into a lush paradise where everything was free, there was no work, and luxury was in perfected abundance. They had no conception of sin nor any familiarity with disobedience of God's orders and its consequences. Nor had they ever before been tempted in any way. . . .

From the point of view of the frightened Adam and Eve, God's wrath is naïvely uncalled for. They do not understand why they should suddenly be extricated from Eden and be subjected to a limited life, full of pain, misery, and evil. They confusedly blamed their sin on everyone but themselves, thus showing that they at least recognized the sin. Still they had difficulty understanding the punishment which they received.

The Relationship Between Books IV and IX in "Paradise Lost"

Milton makes Night and Day symbols of Evil and Good throughout his epic. His use of these symbols in Books IV and

IX presents the key to the differences in the two books. In Book IV Satan enters the earth exposed to "the full-blazing sun." However "the sun was sunk, and . . . night's hemisphere had veiled the horizon round; when Satan . . . at midnight returned . . ." to the earth in Book IX. These basic introductory symbols of light and dark serve notice that either good or bad events will ensue.

Another striking difference in the general atmosphere of Paradise during the course of the two books is the total absence of Heavenly intervention in Book IX. In Book IV Urial, Gabrial, Uzziel, Ithuriel, and Zephon are all responsible for obstructing Satan's path toward evil. However in the later book Satan is able to carry out his plans, completely uninhibited by these Heavenly powers. Here man is left to his own resources and, as we see, they are not enough to prevent the fall.

A comparison of the descriptions of Paradise in Books IV and IX leaves two different impressions. From Book IV we form a mental image of a true paradise. The sumptuousness of the fruits "burnished with golden rind," the freshness of the fountains, and the beauty of the myriad hues of the flowers make an impression of bliss and beauty. The rose without a thorn and the pureness of the air place this paradise of Book IV beyond reality, "a colony of Heaven.". . .

Both at Dartmouth and elsewhere the greatest disagreement over grading is centered, not surprisingly, on the question of where the line is to be drawn between passing and failing. The distance between an E and a D appears to be more considerable than that between any two other grades because of the greatly different consequences of giving one or the other. If a paper is hopelessly bad, there is seldom any problem. But an earnest and conscientious teacher, faced with the necessity of deciding a case that is at all doubtful, will hesitate before choosing the lower grade. In this way the dividing line may become obscured by considerations other than those rising from the quality of the paper. Thus one teacher, mindful that the student whose paper he is reading has been given several E's already, writes at the end: "Believe it or not, I hate to flunk people for mechanical errors, especially when I suspect that they are making a reasonable effort to eliminate them. It seems clear that you made an effort to proofread this paper. . . . I'll give you a D this time, but from now on work like this means an E, and that's a pity because some of your writing is good."

This is what may be called the *therapeutic D*. Undoubtedly it serves a useful purpose and ought not to be proscribed even if it could be. But the practice of giving D's for such reasons does serve to confuse qualitative distinctions between writing that deserves to pass and writing that deserves to fail.

The freshman English courses at Dartmouth, then, are interesting and intellectually demanding courses in standard literature, with considerable required writing in them. They are not courses in composition, except incidentally. The only real point of contact between the literature and the instruction in writing is that the writing assignments are usually based on topics drawn from the works read. The courses make no provision for direct instruction in language, in rhetoric, or in the logic of exposition, though presumably the students are to apply the principles of all these disciplines in arriving at a mastery of expository prose composition.

As a result of the practice in writing and of the criticisms made by teachers both on the papers and in conferences, the students' writing does improve. But one wonders whether, given superior students to start with, a more thorough and systematic approach to teaching writing might not gain even better results, especially in matters involving rhetoric and logic.

The literature instruction in Dartmouth's English 1 and 2 is expertly conducted. The instruction in composition, though enjoying almost ideal conditions of class size and teacher load, often is impaired by the limitations that the prevailing pattern of graduate study in English has imposed on the staff, who have been trained to teach literature and not composition. In laboring under this handicap, Dartmouth is by no means alone; to a large extent every college English department in the nation suffers from it.

In their literary emphasis the Dartmouth courses are typical of a kind of freshman English course often found in the more selective colleges and increasingly found in other institutions as the quality of incoming freshmen continues to rise. That such courses are interesting and of collegiate caliber there can be no doubt. That they are the best way to teach expository composition is less certain.

Chapter 3

Trends in Freshman English

A LOOK AT "PANACEAS"

Teaching young people to write well has always proved so frustratingly difficult, and the methods used so time-consuming and laborious for teacher and student alike, that to many people in this country the problem has seemed to be a kind of standing affront to the American reputation for efficiency. Surely, they have thought, there must be some easy, quick, and fairly painless way to do the job; and they have therefore looked eagerly if often naïvely for pat solutions. Not surprisingly, a great many alleged panaceas for teaching writing have been suggested in the past, especially in the last seventy-five years, since the nation's schools and colleges have been firmly committed to the ideal of trying to educate as many young people as possible. For the longing to find an easy answer becomes urgent in direct proportion to the size of school and college enrollments: the more students there are, the more desperate the problem seems to become. Although, as it has happened, none of these "solutions" has really proved to solve anything, it is instructive to review some of them so as to get a little perspective on those that are being urged on us today.

For the first three-quarters of the nineteenth century, students were made to memorize alleged "Laws of Discourse" on the theory, supported by the prevailing view of psychology, that by so doing they would discipline their mental faculties—the reason, the emotions, the will, etc.—and become good writers with a minimum of composing. But in the 1880s, as college populations grew much larger and more heterogeneous, it became disastrously apparent that the theory was not working. New systems of educational psychology introduced about that time from Europe supported the notion that practice is everything and principles of little account. The eventual result was the "daily theme." First introduced by Barrett Wendell in 1884 at Harvard, by 1890 it was being proposed as the solution to all writing problems. But soon it became clear that few students could find enough grist to grind out five themes a week and few teachers had either the time or the energy to mark the mountains of papers that accumulated. Then came the notion that "the paragraph is the composition in miniature" and what holds for the paragraph holds for the whole composition as well. The rationalization was welcomed by exhausted teachers, and the daily theme became the daily paragraph. This device, too, failed to accomplish all that was hoped for it; most students still wrote poorly.

By the late 1890s, when the study of English literature had become well established in both school and college, some teachers argued eloquently that the only way to learn to write well is to read good literature; that the principles of rhetoric and grammar are only barren formulas, and it is a waste of time to study them directly. But about this time the whole question of teaching writing was further muddled by a growing clamor for correctness as the supreme virtue in composition, and for the next three or four decades composition instruction was largely dominated by exercises in grammar and usage and by sentence diagraming. When it became clear that these activities were having no perceptible effect on the ability of students to write good prose, the principal result was to discredit the study of grammar. About 1940 general semantics was hailed as the answer that everybody had been seeking, and for a decade college freshmen pored over the "abstraction ladder" and learned that cow_1 is not cow_2 is not cow_3. But the extravagant claims made for semantics study quickly proved unfounded; its vogue has now largely passed. In the mid-1940s the communications course appeared as a part of the general education movement and for a time flourished widely. Proponents of the plan argued that combining the study of the four "communication skills"—reading, writing, speaking, listening—in the same course would make both instruction and learning more efficient. Disillusionment came early, and today only a handful of these courses survive out of some 200 that existed at the height of the trend in 1948.

Faced with this long and discouraging record of unsuccessful nostrums, English teachers might be expected to be somewhat wary of glamorous new solutions to the problem of teaching students to write. Probably most of them are, but some appear as optimistic of ultimate solutions as ever. With the encouragement of several of the big foundations, an increasing number of English teachers in schools and colleges are now busily involved with "team-teaching," "lay readers," closed-circuit television, overhead projectors, "resource teachers," "teacher aides," etc., in the hope of "scoring a major breakthrough."

If used intelligently, most of these devices simply make it possible to teach more students with fewer teachers; or to word it another way, to make an inadequate supply of qualified teachers go as far as possible. In so far as they accomplish this end, they offer welcome help to a profession beset with increasing difficulties, but none of them shows promise of greatly accelerating the process of teaching a student to write well or of making the task substantially easier for the student.

Two other innovations, which are considerably more interesting, have recently had ambitious claims made for them. One is the so-called "teaching machine"—or, to use a more inclusive term, "programmed learning." The other is not a device or method but a body of knowledge: structural linguistics. Both are being advanced by some of their more enthusiastic supporters (seldom those who are expert) as panaceas for all the troubles with which the teaching of composition is plagued. Because both are widely misunderstood by many English teachers and by those members of the general public who take a more than casual interest in education, it will be a good idea to consider their claims in some detail.

For the past six or eight years, structural linguistics has been one of the most warmly debated topics at professional meetings of English teachers and in professional journals. Extravagant claims have been made for it which have been disputed with equal extravagance. At the same time, it is evident that structural linguistics is not a mere fad and that it is rapidly gaining ground. It is winning more and more converts among rank-and-file teachers in both school and college, often those who are liveliest and best informed. Half a dozen or more good textbooks are now available for English majors and graduate students, and several texts are on the market that present the subject with some success to high school students and college freshmen.

What is structural linguistics and what are its claims to superiority over the kind of language study that is customarily found in the schools and in college freshman English courses?

The English grammar found today in most school handbooks assumed its present form in the eighteenth century, when the increasing fluidity of social classes created a demand for manuals that would enable people newly risen to a higher social level to acquire new habits of dress and accustom themselves to a new standard of living. The books that then appeared (Lowth's *Short Introduction to English Grammar*, 1762, is one of the best known) were written by men who had little if any knowledge of the earlier history of the language, who were not and indeed could not have been expected to be scholars of language in the modern sense. The serious study of the vernacular had not been customary; such attention had been reserved for Latin, as the language of scholarship. When these authors took up the task of writing grammars of English, not surprisingly they turned to Latin for a model, the most perfect language they knew and the one that enjoyed the highest esteem in learned circles. Noting the high degree of inflection in Latin and contrasting this with the few surviving inflections in English, they concluded that English was suffering decay and resolved to arrest the process. They cherished every irregular verb and all inflected forms of nouns, pronouns, and adjectives; spoke of nominative absolute constructions and identified nonexistent dative and vocative cases in English; frowned on terminal prepositions and strove to pump new life into a moribund subjunctive mode—in short, did all they could to force the grammar of English into the mold of Latin grammar. And, since the people for whom these books were being written hungered for certainty, the books were dogmatic, prescriptive, making little pretense of describing the language as it was but instead laying down a plan for the language as these self-appointed authorities thought it should be. In their view, English grammar as it should be would resemble Latin grammar as much as possible. It is substantially this grammar and this view of language that have dominated school instruction in English for the last 200 years. Most current textbooks, especially in the lower schools, are in this tradition—a tradition that has no defenders today among reputable students of the language and that has had none for many years.

There are overlapping areas between structural grammar and the traditional grammar of the school books; they are not totally different systems. Both deal with inflections, with parts of speech (or "form classes"), with phrasal and clausal structures, with kinds of sentences. The very real differences between them rise from radically different premises and methodologies.

Structural linguistics, according to W. Nelson Francis, one of its leading exponents, "is primarily interested in discovering and describing as concisely and accurately as possible the interrelationships and patterns which make up the intricate structure of languages." [1] It boldly sets out to be a science.

As a science, it is bound to consider the phenomena of language as data to be fully and objectively recorded and classified, then generalized from. With this aim in view, the structural linguist regards the spoken language as primary for two reasons: Spoken language *is* the language, and writing is a means of recording it; and only in the spoken language can the linguist find all the devices that convey meaning—pitch, for example, or stress or pause, which in the written language are inadequately suggested by punctuation marks and such typographical devices as italics. This does not mean that the structural linguist disparages the written form of language. He fully recognizes its importance and is aware also of the significant ways in which it differs from the spoken language.

As a scientist, the linguist tries to be objective in his descriptions of language phenomena, rigidly excluding his own preferences. He will record the forms "Does he not?" "Doesn't he?" and "Don't he?" as all being in common use, and he will note in what social contexts each is usually encountered. But as a linguistic scientist he will not consider it his right to say one is good and another is bad, any more than a botanist would feel called upon to label elm trees or willows or poplars good or bad. One should not conclude that the linguist therefore is a defiler of the well of English; he does *not* say that in language "anything goes." He reports the language habits of the educated as well as those of the less educated, because both varieties are English, both are facts that cannot be blinked; but he

[1] *The Structure of American English*, New York: The Ronald Press Company, 1958, p. 26.

will be the first to say that if one wishes to be regarded as a member
of the educated class, one must conform to the language habits of
that class, which in some respects differ from those of other groups
or classes.

In classifying language data, the structural linguist tries, like any
other scientist, to use the most reliable criteria available and to
establish categories that are as nearly airtight as possible. He finds
school grammar particularly defective on these counts. A favorite
example is the usual definition of the sentence as "a group of words
expressing a complete thought." As Paul Roberts remarks, such
definitions are of almost no practical value because "they are in-
vulnerable statements: one can never conclude an argument about
their truth or falsity, and arguers must end by simply stamping
their feet. It may be true that sentences are groups of words expressing complete thoughts, as it may be true that angels are incorporeal
beings, but such statements can be pursued only to tautology: what
is a complete thought?—that which a sentence expresses; what is an
incorporeal being?—an angel." [2] This definition of a sentence is
based on meaning, which the structuralist regards as the least
satisfactory of the three criteria of classification: form, function,
meaning. In practice, no one identifies sentences according to
whether or not they express "complete thoughts" but rather, in
writing, by structural features, and, in speech, by intonation.

The same difficulties appear in the definitions of several of the
parts of speech—the noun, for instance, which older grammar
usually defines as "the name of a person, place, or thing." "Yet we
identify nouns," says W. Nelson Francis, "not by asking if they
name something but by their positions in expressions and by the
formal marks they carry. In the sentence, 'The slithy toves did gyre
and gimble in the wabe,' any speaker of English knows that 'toves'
and 'wabe' are nouns, though he cannot tell what they name, if
indeed they name anything. How does he know? Actually because
they have certain formal marks, like their position in relation to
'the' as well as the whole arrangement of the sentence."

Francis goes on to criticize not only school grammar's use of
meaning as a principal criterion of classification but also its failure
to use it consistently.

[2] "The Relation of Linguistics to the Teaching of English," *College English*,
22:2, 1960.

It shifts the ground of its classification and produces the elementary logical error of cross-division. A zoologist who divided animals into invertebrates, mammals, and beasts of burden would not get very far before running into trouble. Yet the traditional grammar is guilty of the same error when it defines three parts of speech on the basis of meaning (noun, verb, and interjection), four more on the basis of function (adjective, adverb, pronoun, conjunction), and one partly on function and partly on form (preposition). The result is that in such an expression as "a dog's life" there can be endless futile argument about whether "dog's" is a noun or an adjective. It is, of course, a noun from the point of view of form and an adjective from the point of view of function, and hence falls into both classes, just as a horse is both a mammal and a beast of burden.[3]

The structural linguist adheres strictly to form as a criterion of classification, since it is the most objective aspect of language and therefore the most satisfactory for his purposes. Using this criterion he identifies four principal devices that English employs to indicate structural meaning (in contrast to the lexical meaning conveyed by individual words considered outside a context). The first is word order, highly important in a language with few inflections (compare "Williams caught the shark" with "The shark caught Williams"). The second is "function words," words such as articles, prepositions, and conjunctions whose purpose is to indicate structural relationships. Third is inflections (*man, man's, men, men's; sing, sings, sang, sung; hot, hotter, hottest;* etc.). Last is "formal alteration," changes in form indicating changes in function (the difference among *educate, educational, educator, education,* etc.). When the linguist analyzes spoken language, he identifies a fifth kind of device, variations in pitch, stress, and juncture (pause), all of which indicate structural meaning (compare "What's this in the meat loaf, Sarah?" with "What's this in the meat loaf—Sarah?").

In keeping with this analysis of structure, the structuralist reduces the number of "parts of speech," usually to four plus the general category of function words. C. C. Fries goes so far as to designate these four main groups with new names: Class 1, Class 2, Class 3,

[3] "Revolution in Grammar," reprinted in Harold B. Allen, ed., *Readings in Applied English Linguistics*, New York: Appleton-Century-Crofts, Inc., 1958, pp. 53–54. Originally published in *Quarterly Journal of Speech*, 40:299–312, 1954.

and Class 4, since they do not correspond exactly with the traditional categories.[4] Other structuralists, however, recognizing that these four groups are roughly equivalent to what have been called *substantives, verbs, adjectives,* and *adverbs,* have retained the old names but redefined them.

This is not the place to go into the details of structural grammar, which like any comprehensive description of a language is lengthy and complex. Most of the prominent structural linguists have written semipopular essays describing their discipline,[5] as well as textbooks for teaching it. It is enough to say here that more and more English teachers at all levels are finding this view of the language convincing, though they may have struggled against it at first, as Paul Roberts reports that he did. Trained originally as a medievalist (as many of the present generation of linguists were), Roberts says that when he first became aware of linguistics, he opposed it and wanted to defend the tradition he was familiar with. "But when I tried to, I found the tradition largely indefensible. I found myself giving ground, grudgingly but steadily, until I was forced to the realization that the picture of the language I was giving my students was false—not false in all its details, but false as a whole, falsely grounded. I had then some painful questions to answer." [6]

Structural grammar continues to meet a great deal of resistance that is due simply to inertia, prejudice, and lack of information. But it has also come under attack lately by exponents of an equally rigorous scientific system of language study, the so-called "transformation" grammar. Developed initially by Noam Chomsky and introduced in a little book called *Syntactic Structures* in 1957, it is rapidly gaining support among language theorists and seems certain to force a number of changes in structuralist theory, though few expect it to supplant structural grammar. It is difficult to say anything about this system in a sentence or two and give any clear

[4] *The Structure of English,* New York: Harcourt, Brace & World, Inc., 1952, pp. 113–141.

[5] See especially Sumner Ives, "Linguistics in the Classroom," *College English,* 17:165–172, 1955; W. Nelson Francis, "Revolution in Grammar"; Paul Roberts, "The Relation of Linguistics to the Teaching of English"; Henry Lee Smith, *Linguistic Science and the Teaching of English,* Inglis Lecture, Cambridge, Mass.: Harvard University Press, 1956.

[6] *Patterns of English,* Teacher's Edition, New York: Harcourt, Brace & World, Inc., 1956, p. 2.

notion of its distinguishing characteristics. About the most anyone can say in this space is that it attempts to describe the English language by identifying a limited number of "kernel" sentences ("simple, declarative, active, with no complex verb or noun phrases") [7] and, by the application of a relatively small number of rules which "transform" the kernel sentences into more complicated structures, to "generate" all possible sentences in English. The process can also be reversed: the grammarian can determine the structure of given sentences by applying to them the transformation rules.

One respect in which transformation grammar has an advantage over structural grammar can be illustrated by two phrases that Chomsky analyzes, "the growling of lions" and "the raising of flowers." [8] According to structural grammar these phrases are identical, both consisting of a gerund modified by a prepositional phrase. Yet a native speaker of English will sense intuitively that in spite of their apparent similarity the phrases are somehow different. Chomsky explains the difference by pointing out that each is a transformation of a different kernel sentence, "the growling of lions" being a transformation of "lions growl" and "the raising of flowers" of "John [or someone] raises flowers." Structural grammar at present is unable to take account of such differences.

When one considers the argument now going on between structuralists and transformationists, as well as the continuing arguments among structuralists themselves as they try to standardize their terminology and methods, the present situation of English grammar admittedly looks confusing. If the study of English grammar is in such a state of turmoil and change, some people may say, perhaps we had better stay with the good old-fashioned grammar of the handbooks until things have settled down and we can know which group is right. Unfortunately, if one accepts the premise that grammar deserves to be taught at all, such a policy will hardly serve. The clock can neither be turned back nor permanently stopped. English teachers for the most part have been teaching a static system of grammar, one that reflects almost no awareness of the enormous amount of scholarly investigation of language during the last three-quarters of a century and more, or of the revolution that language study has undergone in the last thirty years. Parents would

[7] Noam Chomsky, *Syntactic Structures,* 's Gravenhage: Mouton and Co., 1957, p. 107.

[8] Chomsky, *op. cit.,* pp. 88–89.

rightly be shocked to learn that their children were studying psychology or physics under teachers and out of textbooks that were untouched by an awareness of developments in those fields since 1900. Yet this is very close to the situation that has existed—that largely still exists—with respect to the study of English grammar.

What is happening now is that English teachers are suddenly beginning to be pushed into the position that their colleagues in the social and natural sciences have been familiar with for a long time. The latter have learned to live with change and indeed to regard it as an assurance that their subjects are alive and flourishing. A new textbook on physics may become out of date in some respects between the time its author completes the manuscript and the time it is published a year later; but physics teachers would not argue that new textbooks on physics should therefore be prohibited until research in physics tapers off or until all the ultimate truths about physics have been revealed. The study of English grammar *is* in an unsettled state nowadays, but this should be a cause for satisfaction, not dismay.

Whether or not structural grammar is correct in all its details, there is no question that it presents a vastly truer picture of the English language and its modes of working than traditional schoolbook grammar does. Here is reason enough for preferring it. But what other advantages does it offer? Can it, for example, be expected to revolutionize the teaching of English composition and make easy what has been so difficult? The answer is no. This discipline has revolutionized the teaching of English as a foreign language by furnishing the foreign student an accurate picture of the ways in which English operates, and by stressing the primary importance of gaining an oral command of basic patterns before proceeding to the conscious study of grammar and of the written language. But the native American student from first grade on already has a fluent oral command of English, and by the time he is ready to study grammar and composition, he has already had considerable experience with reading it and at least some with writing it. The two situations are not comparable.[9]

[9] W. F. Twaddell has pointed out that the English teacher as teacher of composition tries to make his students *bi-dialectal* and is mainly concerned with those aspects of English grammar that set off written from spoken English, formal from casual, standard from substandard. The foreign-language

It has long been known that the study of school grammar has little or no perceptible effect on the student's ability to write good prose. It may or may not help him to write more correctly, but correctness is only the absence of error, a negative virtue, important but by no means synonymous with quality in writing. Whether structural grammar will have a more appreciable effect on composition skill remains to be seen. So far no child has been taught his native English from this point of view from the first grade through the twelfth, and until considerable evidence of this sort is available, the ultimate effects of the new approach can only be guessed at.

Responsible linguists themselves make no claims that their subject will solve the problems of teaching students to write well. They say that as a truer description of the structure of English, structural grammar deserves to be taught; no teacher should knowingly present inaccurate information to his students under the guise of its being accurate. They point also to the greater interest consistently aroused in students by this kind of grammar. Unlike school grammar, which presents them with contradictions, inaccurate generalizations, and arbitrary statements that they must take on trust, structural grammar is systematic and tries to furnish rational answers to students' questions about language. It makes sense. But

---

teacher, however, tries to make his students *bilingual* and is therefore concerned with almost entirely different aspects of English grammar. "That which conflicts most persistently with the new foreign-language grammatical habits of our learners," Twaddell says, "is the 'deep grammar' of English—those features which are common to spoken *and* written, to casual *and* formal, to sub-standard *and* standard English, simply because they are all English." If an English composition teacher were to find one of his students writing "a girl good-looking" or "Works Mr. Walsh in Mr. Stone's shop?" he would know at once that the trouble lay not in a confusion of spoken and written English, casual and formal, or substandard and standard, but rather with a conflict caused by the student's familiarity with the grammar of some other language. No native speaker of English makes this kind of error. Twaddell goes on to say that if the English composition teacher were to teach linguistics, this knowledge would make the foreign language teacher's job that much easier; but he does not claim that it would directly benefit the teaching of English composition.

Twaddell's article, entitled "Does the Foreign-language Teacher Have to Teach English Grammar?" appeared in *Publications of the Modern Language Association of America,* 77:18–22, 1962.

above all, linguists will defend the study of the new grammar on the ground that it presents information that is intrinsically valuable, worth knowing for its own sake. Like the study of literature or mathematics or geography, the study of one's language has general cultural value quite apart from whatever practical value may result —or even if no practical value results.

Some linguists will, when urged, express a few tentative hopes for possible direct effects of linguistic study on a student's writing. One is that a familiarity with the principal patterns of pitch, stress, and juncture in spoken English (what the linguist calls "supra-segmental phonemes") should help a student punctuate more accurately. Sentence fragments and comma faults, for example, are not really errors in sentence structure but errors in punctuation; comma faults and sentence fragments are no problem in speech, for intonation contours and pauses clearly mark the end of one statement and the beginning of the next. The difference between restrictives and nonrestrictives can also be better approached through a study of the different contours that mark the utterance of the two kinds of element than through confusing attempts to differentiate the two by meaning. Linguists will point out that the troubles that students have with English spelling cannot be ended by linguistics or indeed by anything short of a new alphabet; but by making clearer the relation between the spoken language and our mode of symbolizing it in writing, linguistics may at least help to make the nature of the problem apparent and to rationalize it to some extent—a gain, though admittedly a small one. Finally, linguists will express the belief that a fuller and more accurate understanding of English sentence structure *may* help indirectly to increase the student's control over sentence patterns in his own writing. And, just as the study of literature should make a student more sensitive to the uses of words, so should the study of an accurate grammar of English make him more aware of the nature of the instrument he uses every day. No direct carryover from either literature or language study to writing skill has been demonstrated, but it is reasonable to believe that neither is irrelevant to writing skill.

It seems idle, then, to hope that linguistics will prove a panacea for composition teaching. As Sumner Ives has said, linguistics "does not cover all the things that the composition teacher needs to know. There is still no royal road to good writing, no magic method that will turn out skilled writers, and neither linguistics nor any other field is likely to provide one."[10]

Programmed instruction—with or without the hardware of teaching machines—is a method of teaching based on the behavioral principle of reinforcement. B. F. Skinner, the psychologist who has had the most to do with the modern development of programming, contends that by making use of what is known of the learning processes of both human and subhuman organisms, students can learn subject matters and skills as well as they do now but with less time and energy; or, more important, that with the same or less expenditure of time and energy, they can learn a great deal more.

Programming entails both a method of preparing material to be learned and a method of presenting this material to the student. Since it is the latter that has been receiving most of the publicity, perhaps it is the better place to begin.

A teaching machine or a programmed text is a device that presents one item or frame at a time; that is, it allows students to see one sentence with a critical word left out or one statement followed by a question. The student writes the required answer on the program itself or on an answer tape or booklet. If he has been using a typical teaching machine, he then activates a mechanism that moves his answer under a clear plastic window (where he cannot change it) at the same time that it reveals the correct answer. The student then indicates whether he was right or wrong and again activates the machine to reveal the next item. The same procedure, in non-mechanized form, is followed in a programmed text. Either the student keeps the correct answer covered while he writes his own answer and then compares them or the correct answer is printed on the page following the item, and the student turns the page to see the correct answer after he has written his own.

This description applies to "linear" or Skinnerian programs; that is, those programs in which a student starts at item one and composes or constructs his answer to every item in the program. The other major kind of programs is called "branching" and is exemplified most clearly by "scrambled books." Here the student reads a rather large block of information followed by a question. He then chooses an answer from among several. Each answer refers him to a different page number. If he chooses the correct answer, he is told

[10] Ives, *op. cit.*, p. 172.

that he is right and he is given another piece of information, another question, and another choice of answers each with a corresponding page number. If the student chooses the wrong answer, he is referred to a page on which he is told he is wrong and on which the relevant information is clarified for him.

Two of the requirements of programmed instruction are met by all teaching machines and all programmed books. First, unlike the television class or the lecture, programs require the active participation of each student at every step. It is impossible for a student to work through a program passively. Unlike even a small class situation, in a programmed presentation the instructor knows what answer every student would give to every question, not just the answers of the students called on in class. Second, and more central to the theoretical basis of programming, is the immediate knowledge that a student has of whether his responses were right.

The theory that underlies programmed instruction is that when an organism acts so as to bring about any change in its environment, that change in turn affects the organism. All other things being equal, if the change made on the environment satisfies a need of the organism, the fact of the satisfaction increases the likelihood that the behavior that produced it will recur. Much of Skinner's work has been done on animals that are kept below their body weight, which means that food acts as a potent "reinforcer" of the behavior that the experimenter wants the organism to produce. In carefully controlled experiments Skinner and others have found that the sooner reinforcement follows the desired behavior, the more rapidly an organism will learn and the more likely it is that that behavior will be produced again.

Under less rigorous conditions, parents, teachers, and pet-owners use the same techniques, offering rewards to encourage the behavior they want from children, students, and dalmatians. Since a programmer cannot reduce his student to 80 per cent of normal body weight and feed him when an item is answered correctly, he must rely on other kinds of rewards to reinforce the behavior he wants. Skinner's assumption is that in our culture "being right," and knowing that one is right, is reinforcing.

It is easy to meet these first two requirements of programming: having students make overt responses and letting them know at once whether their responses are correct or not. It is the other requirements that present obstacles, some of which may prove insurmountable in the teaching of certain subjects. For a program to succeed, the programmer must first specify precisely the behavior he wants. Having specified that behavior exactly, he must work out a rigorous presentation of material that will enable the learner to participate actively at every step. The steps of the program, often many thousands, must be so devised that the student is right almost all of the time (since it is assumed that being right is reinforcing). They must also progress in a completely logical sequence in very small steps to lead the student inductively from the simple skills and knowledge that he already has to the complex skills and knowledge that the programmer has set as the goal of the program.

Because gadgetry is easier to produce than intelligent teaching programs, perhaps as many as 200 teaching machines of one kind or another are now on the market, whereas courses of instruction to be used in these machines have been much slower to appear and good programs even slower. Programs have, however, been prepared in subjects as diverse as introductory psychology, high school physics, parts of elementary foreign language, statistics, school mathematics, logic, histology, and linguistics.

Supported by grants from foundations and branches of the Federal government, some schools and colleges are beginning to give a great deal of attention to preparing programs. Textbook publishers too have become excited about the possibilities of "automated instruction," and nearly every important house appears to have teams of people busy writing programs. Some of this activity is being directed toward aspects of the English curriculum. Spelling so far is receiving the most attention, though programs also exist or are being prepared for vocabulary building (junior high school level), elementary reading, grammar of various kinds, and poetry. Several universities have let it be known that they are "programming remedial English composition," but on examination it turns out that they are seldom attempting anything so ambitious. One such project has simply been programming traditional workbook grammar and usage—elementary exercises on apostrophes, agreement, pronoun reference, and similar mechanical matters. This is not the same thing as "programming English composition," remedial or otherwise. Another is attempting to program the same sort of material but is using some of the terminology and assumptions of structural linguistics, as far as these apply to the limited objective in mind, which is simply to enable remedial students to pass a standard objective test in grammar, usage, and mechanics.

At a recent convention of college English teachers, one young man reported that he has been "programming rhetoric." A glance at the handout he had brought with him proved that he was indeed programming rhetoric but not in a way that will prove widely useful in teaching English composition: he had prepared a list of twenty-nine figures of speech, from anaphora to hyperbaton to prosopopoeia, and was drilling students in their spelling, derivation, and definition. The United States Office of Education is supporting several projects that are attempting to program information drawn from structural or transformational linguistics, but improvement in composition skill is not an overt aim of these projects. One "programmed textbook" intended for English composition courses has been on the market for several years and has already undergone one revision. It is not really a textbook on composition, however, but one on old-fashioned school grammar and punctuation—a much narrower matter.

So far, spelling is the only aspect of composition teaching where programming has appeared to be clearly superior to present methods of instruction, and the evidence even here is still far from complete. There is a good reason why spelling should lend itself to programming. The goal of instruction in spelling can be clearly and unequivocally specified: the student is to be taught to spell a given word in only one way. The goal is correctness according to a rigid standard. The student's success or lack of it can be easily determined: the word is rightly spelled or it is not. No element of personal judgment enters in.

It seems likely that some aspects of conventional grammar and mechanics will also prove susceptible of being programmed. Again, the "behavioral outcome" that is desired can be clearly specified for some of these matters. Subjects should agree with verbs, pronouns with antecedents; declarative sentences should end with periods, interrogative sentences with question marks; and so on.

Students can be instructed in these conventions at any length that seems necessary so that they will come to recognize errors in them when they appear in the programmed material and be able to correct the errors. The usual English workbooks do this much. But whereas workbook instruction has never carried over very successfully to the student's own composition habits, machine instruction may succeed somewhat better because of the immediate-feedback principle (the student learns at once whether his answer is right or wrong) and because it may be possible to present the information in some kind of planned sequence that will facilitate learning.

But beyond the elementary usages mentioned above—and they are fewer than one might think—the particular behavioral outcome that is wanted begins to appear less clear-cut. Take for example the use of a comma after an introductory adverbial element in a sentence, which at first glance seems a simple enough matter. The difficulty is that one does not customarily use a comma after *every* adverbial opener, only those that are "fairly long or complicated" or those that need a comma to prevent misreading or ambiguity. Exactly how long is "fairly long"? When does such an element become "fairly complicated"? Does a three-word opener require a comma? One of four words? What principle leads one to see that a given opener is ambiguous or that it is in danger of being misread? In practice, when a student is writing a sentence in a composition and he has to decide whether or not to use a comma in this kind of situation, there is unfortunately no clear-cut standard of right or wrong to guide him as there is in spelling. He must decide on the evidence furnished by the particular sentence, considered both in itself and in its relation to the style of the whole composition— whether the style is of the formal kind that favors close punctuation or the less formal in which open punctuation is appropriate. Many other aspects of "mechanics" involve even more difficult choices in which a sophisticated feeling for style is necessary, a cultivated sense of good taste and rhetorical effect. For example, how does one decide when to use a semicolon between two main clauses, rather than a period or a dash or even a colon?

But the mechanical aspects of writing are essentially superficial; teaching their correct use, difficult though it may often be, is not synonymous with teaching composition. When someone teaches composition, he is trying to cultivate in the student a bafflingly complex intellectual skill. Instruction in it does not proceed in a systematic and sequential way, where one thing must be learned before the next can be understood; instead, a student needs all things at once whenever he composes anything as long as a paragraph. This lack of clear sequence is bound to be a severe handicap for anyone trying to program English composition in any rounded sense. It may make success impossible.

Even more difficult of solution will be the problem of trying to specify clear goals for programmed instruction in composition. In the most general terms, the goal should be to help the student "write well." But what does this mean? Correctness is obviously one part of writing well, and its presence or absence is fairly easy to determine. But correctness alone does not make good writing. A student who writes well must have something to say and must say it effectively. No specific answer is possible to the question of what "something to say" may mean in all circumstances; it depends, among other things, on the quality of the student's mind and on the amount and kind of furniture in it. Effectiveness can be broken down more easily. By effective writing we mean writing that is well organized; that shows an awareness of a particular group of intended readers and is shaped with their needs in mind; that contains unified and well-developed paragraphs of fitting length, well-made sentences showing a due variety in length and structure, words thoughtfully chosen with attention to both their denotative and connotative meanings. All these aspects should add up to a style, an impression of a consistent point of view and distinct personality behind the composition.

But there is no clear general principle for writing well-made sentences composed of well-chosen words. One cannot set up as the desired behavioral outcome of a programmed unit on the sentence that the student should at the end of the unit be able to write well-made sentences. The goal is too general, covering an enormous range of possibilities in order to take account of the infinite number of possible sentences that might be written. The goal can be broken down, of course, into instruction in such things as parallelism, balance, rhythm, unity, emphatic placement of sentence elements, variety and length of structure, periodicity, etc. These are the principles of sentence rhetoric. Can programmed instruction do a better job of teaching them to a student than present methods, which though not wholly fruitless have clearly not been uniformly successful? The answer cannot be known with certainty until a great deal more experimentation has been carried out, but meanwhile there is little cause for great optimism.

Consider parallel structure as an example. A carefully written program on parallelism should be able to teach a student what parallel structure is, how to recognize it, how to check it for accuracy, how to correct instances of faulty parallelism. If successful, it should help him to avoid errors in parallelism in his own writing. But can such a program enable the student to know when it is appropriate or effective to use parallel structure in his own writing and when it is not; what kinds of sentence elements should be put in parallel in a given instance—prepositional phrases, infinitives, clauses, single words; the point at which parallelism ceases to be a useful rhetorical device and becomes a mannerism? All these considerations are determined by the relationship of the ideas being expressed in the sentence, the audience addressed, the writer's purpose, the degree of emphasis desired, the rhythm and euphony of the sentence, above all the writer's *taste*, which is a direct reflection of himself. All of these are variables, unpredictable except within limits so broad as to be nearly without meaning. The number of their possible combinations is infinite. If rhetoric were a science instead of an art, principles and laws could be discovered that would dictate choice at every step; but since it is an art, its principles are based on other premises and presuppose a large degree of subjectivity in their application.

How is parallelism customarily taught in English courses now? If it is taught (and many students are never asked to study it), there is probably some discussion of the principles underlying parallel structure, analysis of prose selections to illustrate parallelism, perhaps assigned reading in a rhetorical handbook, the working of some exercises on parallelism. The conscientious teacher will then assign a theme and require that the students consciously make some use of parallel structure in their papers; when he marks the papers, he will be especially alert to identify examples of it, to criticize ineffective and commend successful uses.

How well does this method work? It is hard to say. Whether a student has studied parallelism in the way just described or has studied it with the help of a teaching machine or programmed textbook, measuring the degree of his success in using parallelism is difficult. By studying a sample of his writing, one can determine with certainty whether or not he has made use of parallelism at all; and if he has, whether any of the parallel structures are incorrectly put together. But the central question of whether he has used parallelism effectively—and if so, how effectively—must be answered subjectively. And at that point disagreement begins, for there is no way to get complete unanimity on such matters. In any case, one cannot be entirely sure that any gain that may be noted is due entirely to the formal instruction and not to some unknown outside influence.

What this all comes down to is that teaching composition by conventional methods is admittedly difficult and often inefficient; we cannot be objectively sure of the success of these methods, though we may have strong subjective convictions about how well or ill they are working. Although programmed instruction may offer hope of greater efficiency in teaching some things such as spelling and mechanics, there is considerable doubt that composition in a real sense can be taught any better by this method. Programmed instruction is especially suitable for giving a student command of the data of an organized body of knowledge such as psychology or arithmetic or physics, and an *understanding* of this body of knowledge. But composition is not a body of knowledge; instead it is a highly complex skill—perhaps the most complex of all human skills. It seems likely that the behavior patterns involved in writing well are too complex to be isolated one by one and systematically programmed for machine instruction. This is only hypothesis, however, not fact. Five or ten years of extensive experimentation by many people are needed to explore the possibility of improving composition skill through programmed instruction. But enough is known now of the complexity of the writing process and the limitations of this kind of instruction to discourage all but the most sanguine Skinnerian from expecting teaching machines to be a panacea for English composition. They may be able to relieve the composition teacher of some of his more elementary chores and for this reason alone deserve the most thoughtful study. But the teacher of composition, uncertain though he may be of exactly how successful his efforts are and unable to agree on just how writing should be taught, is still the most complicated and versatile of all teaching machines and therefore unlikely to be displaced.

THE NEXT FIVE YEARS

The trends now visible in freshman English have some significance for the probable future of this course in most four-year colleges and universities. As mentioned in an earlier chapter, remedial English courses (except in the junior colleges) have been declining rapidly, and the decline is accelerating. Where the course still exists, it is commonly regarded frankly as subcollegiate and the student taking it is penalized in one way or another. The so-called "review of fundamentals," a traditional feature of the freshman course, is being dropped at many colleges. The student is asked instead to correct his own mistakes with the help of his handbook or by voluntarily attending a writing clinic. A few years ago attendance at such clinics was often compulsory for weak students, but the tendency now is to put the student on his own. On the basis of a limited survey of textbooks now in use, there is some evidence of a preference for the more difficult and more scholarly handbooks and books of readings—ones that four or five years ago were found more often in small honors sections than in those for the majority of students. At colleges where the increase in quality of students has been marked, writing clinics have been discontinued, since students now are seldom so poorly prepared as to require special remedial services of this sort. Finally, as special provisions for the dull or poorly prepared students have dwindled, those for the best students have multiplied. Through exemption from normal course requirements or through specially devised honors courses, these students are now the objects of a solicitous regard, whereas a few years ago they were often lumped together with run-of-the-mill students and allowed to coast along as they chose.

In all of these changes, one can detect the outlines of a pattern emerging. Ten or fifteen years ago it was usual to find at, say, a state university a full-fledged remedial course (often conferring credit); a lengthy "review" of grammar, usage, and mechanics in the first semester of the regular freshman course; and a writing clinic or laboratory. The marginal student was most carefully attended to and nursed along as far as he could be induced to go; it was much less common to find the superior student being given a comparable amount of attention. Today in colleges where there has been the greatest improvement in the caliber of entering freshmen, it appears that the remedial course is the first to go; then the regular freshman course is freed from the "review of fundamentals"; next the writing clinic is dropped; and in a few instances freshman composition itself has in effect disappeared, being replaced by a course in literature with a certain amount of required writing. It seems likely that this is the way most four-year institutions are now headed, and they will move in this direction just as fast as the caliber of their students will permit them to.

These are major changes, ones that only a few years ago would have been thought visionary. They have come about because of a general and substantial rise in the average level of ability and of preparation among entering freshmen these past four or five years. What accounts for this rise? There appear to be two reasons for it.

The first is simply that the number of young people who want to attend college is expanding at a considerably faster rate than are freshman class enrollments at four-year colleges and universities. As a result, most colleges can now be more selective in their choice of applicants. Even those colleges that still accept all comers find their rate of expansion limited by facilities and staff. But most four-year institutions have either raised their entrance requirements or imposed such requirements for the first time; if barred by statute from imposing entrance requirements, they are finding other ways to identify poor students ahead of time and dissuade them from enrolling.

One of the most important influences, of course, is the proliferation of junior colleges throughout the nation, which are siphoning off many of the weaker students. It is important to recognize that the sharp decline of remedial English courses in four-year colleges and universities does not signify a phenomenal rise in intellectual force among the younger generation, nor does it mean that the high schools at last have solved the problem of teaching all students to write well. The students who used to populate remedial English courses in the colleges and universities are still with us, but most of them now appear to be going to junior colleges instead of to the more selective institutions. A recent survey by the National Council of Teachers of English showed that in 1960–1961 some 10 million dollars was being spent for remedial English in the nation's colleges; half of this sum was being spent in the junior colleges.[11]

The other reason why the colleges are now getting better freshmen than they did three or four years ago is that the high schools, though they have not found a panacea for teaching writing, are doing a better job of preparing students in English. How much better it is still hard to say, but freshman English directors around the country seem generally to agree that the improvement is a fact—pronounced in some states, barely perceptible in others, but apparent nevertheless.

Behind this improved preparation lie a number of developments that have begun to have a favorable effect on English teaching in the schools, and other developments are pending that will hasten the trend.

One of these developments is a sharp change in the educational philosophy that undergirds the high school curriculum. It is a swing away from "whole child," "life adjustment" education toward a philosophy of greater intellectual rigor in the teaching of academic subjects. This change had its beginnings in the 1940s but has been gaining momentum rapidly in the last five or six years. The climate in the high schools is now hospitable to more work and harder work, and the study of English has inevitably benefited to a degree.

Partly as a result of the changed climate and partly because of popular clamor and of criticism from the colleges, students have lately been doing more writing in their high school English classes. There has been some progress here and there in reducing class size so that teachers have a better chance of correcting their students' papers with thoroughness; and the growth of the lay reader plan has also served to encourage more writing.

Although the number of freshmen who receive Advanced Placement credit in English is still very small, more and more students are taking Advanced Placement courses in high school and presenting this work to the colleges for validation. Perhaps the most significant effects of the Advanced Placement Program in English so far have been to establish a precedent in the colleges for exempting unusually well-prepared students from the customary freshman require-

[11] *The National Interest and the Teaching of English*, National Council of Teachers of English, Committee on National Interest, Champaign, Ill., 1961, p. 112.

ments and to tone up high school instruction by establishing a new and higher ceiling for achievement.

Finally, major efforts are now being undertaken to upgrade the teaching of English in the schools in much the same way that instruction in science, mathematics, and foreign language has recently been improved. The Commission on English of the College Entrance Examination Board sponsored institutes on twenty university campuses in the summer of 1962 at which 900 high school teachers took graduate courses in literature, language, and composition. The United States Office of Education has initiated "Project English," which is promoting research to improve the English curriculum at all levels. Six "Curriculum Study Centers" have already been established as a part of this program. Each of these will spend up to five years working out sequential curricula in English and writing curricular materials to be tried out in the classroom. Many local and regional projects, some of them of great scope and consequence, have also been undertaken and will soon make their influence widely felt—projects in Pittsburgh, in Westport, Connecticut, in Lincoln, Nebraska, in Portland, Oregon, and elsewhere.

As a result of these developments in the high schools and of more selective enrollment, it seems certain that the improvement that has lately been noticed in the English preparation of entering freshmen is bound to continue. The changes already mentioned in freshman English courses are evidence of some adjustment to these changed conditions, but so far there is little sign of a really searching reevaluation of the English courses of the freshman and sophomore years and their relation to the English curriculum of the schools. If college English departments continue to delay such a reassessment of their own courses, they are likely within less than five years to find themselves in the unaccustomed position of having major changes forced upon them by the lower schools.

To take one example, an almost invariable feature of the most ambitious and best-planned projects for upgrading English instruction in the schools nowadays is the firm determination to introduce up-to-date knowledge about language into the curriculum—not merely correct usage but the principles of English structure, the relation of speech to writing, information about American dialects and linguistic geography, something of the history of English. This material is not being recommended mainly as a practical aid to composition but rather as humane knowledge worth studying for its own sake, for what it can reveal about man as a communicating creature. A few freshman English courses have been moving in this direction too, but the high schools are plainly in the lead in this important development. It is safe to predict that in not more than five years many colleges and universities will be getting substantial numbers of freshmen who have had the benefit of this kind of instruction and who will find the traditional prescriptive grammar naïve and inaccurate. To avoid acute public embarrassment, the colleges will be obliged to update their own courses and textbooks and to retrain their freshman English staffs. Or they can, of course, ignore classroom instruction in language and teach only literature, but this plan will have its difficulties too. If high school English can give a rounded and up-to-date view of both language and literature, many will ask, why is it that college English must confine itself only to the study of literature?

Assuming that the trends just mentioned will continue, what is likely to happen with respect to the freshman English course? In the great majority of those colleges where the force of these trends is strongly felt, it seems probable that English departments will convert the freshman composition course into one in literature with, as they will hasten to say, "required assignments in writing." This moving away from the study of language and rhetoric toward the study of literature represents the natural bias of most college English teachers; their training in both undergraduate and graduate study has been preponderantly literary, so it is not surprising that they should prefer to teach what they know most about. And as mentioned earlier, there is no question that an English composition course based on literature has many advantages over one based on the kind of dilute sociological survey that many of the freshman English anthologies encourage. The teacher knows what he is talking about, he is likely to be enthusiastic about the subject matter, and the students have something to write about that the teacher is qualified to pass judgment on. The trouble is that literature has such a sirenlike attractiveness for English teachers that most of them find it hard to remember that they have any obligation to teach anything else. The literature drives out less glamorous subject matter, and composition is either forgotten or taught incidentally and grudgingly. The principles of good writing may surely be deduced from examples of the best writing, but few English teachers choose to try. As one freshman English director has remarked, "The real advantage of putting literature in the freshman course is that it makes the teachers so happy."

If one were inclined to be cynical, one might suspect that the required writing in the sort of reconstituted freshman composition course that has been mentioned is likely to be at least in part a rationalization, window dressing for the benefit of the general faculty who years ago voted to grant the English department a fourth or a fifth of every student's freshman schedule to improve his command of the mother tongue. The mention of required writing minimizes the risk of losing this block of time and of putting the course on the same elective footing as other courses in the humanities.

There are lessons implicit in the present state of freshman English, and they are pointed straight at college English departments. Though perfection in the teaching of English in the high schools is still a long way off, major efforts are now being undertaken to bring about fundamental reforms in the English curriculum of the schools, to rationalize it and bring it into line with current knowledge as has been done so successfully in the teaching of science and mathematics and foreign languages. But when one takes a close look at the freshman English courses which nearly half of all the young people graduating from high school will take, it becomes painfully evident that the muddle in the college course is scarcely better than the one that college teachers have deplored in high school English courses, with the sobering difference that so far almost nothing is being done in the colleges to reform the freshman course. There is no widespread impulse to think through afresh the premises and purposes of this course (or perhaps one should say to think them through for the first time); to mesh it with instruction in the high schools and make it the end link in a chain instead of an isolated phenomenon; to anticipate and prepare for important changes that are imminent in the English curriculum of the schools; to offer instruction in prose composition at an intellectual level compatible with college or university study. Instead, college English departments seem increasingly willing to abandon the responsibility for giving systematic instruction in composition just as soon as a majority of entering freshmen show themselves able to observe a minimum standard of correctness in written English—as though mere correctness were all that one should try to teach in a composition course, as though correct writing were necessarily the same as good writing.

There are quite as many things wrong with freshman English in college as with English in high school, and it is just as urgent that something be done about them. Some of the weaknesses of the college course are undoubtedly the result of its having to remedy (or try to remedy) deficiencies of earlier instruction. But most of them arise from a vast uncertainty about aims, about content, about methods—the same uncertainty that has afflicted the teaching of English in high school. It will no longer be enough for college English professors to point out the defects of English instruction in the high schools, even when (as sometimes happens) they are willing to work side by side with high school teachers to help set things right. College English departments must begin also to look nearer home for imperfection: it appears to be the old problem of the mote and the beam. And with the growing number of projects aimed at improving the teaching of English in high school, the colleges can ill afford to delay.

Chapter 4

The Writing of College Students After the Freshman Year

ENGLISH PROFICIENCY AT DARTMOUTH

Not all students can be taught to write with distinction, or even to write equally well. One should no more expect every student to earn an A in English composition than one should expect every student to earn an A in chemistry or algebra or German. Differences in aptitude, in background, and in degree of interest will always ensure variations in the degree of skill that students are able to attain. Yet there can be little doubt that the great majority of students who enroll at reputable four-year colleges and universities are entirely capable of learning to write, if not with distinction, at least with a decent regard for correctness and clarity. Those who are not— who are unable to master the simple conventions of correct writing or to impose some degree of order on their mental processes—have no place in an institution devoted to *higher* education.

An English department, in its required freshman English courses, can diagnose a student's writing difficulties for him, acquaint him with the principles that he is violating or needs to observe (the principles of grammar, usage, rhetoric, logic), and provide a *limited* amount of disciplined practice in writing. At the end of the sequence, the department can point to the papers written by the student and say that he is able at this point in his educational career to write at the level of quality that they exemplify. He can, that is, if he wants to, or if he is persuaded that he must.

But an English department cannot guarantee that the student will continue to write this well forever, or even next year, or even next hour in another course. The behavior patterns involved in writing well are so numerous, so complex, so much a part of all the other aspects of a student's intellectual life that these patterns must be constantly reinforced during all a student's years of schooling if they finally are to become habitual. The point was well made in a little book on education published a decade ago:

> The ability to organize and express ideas is not a skill which is acquired at a given age and then simply put to use; it is a function of the total growth of the mind and must develop as experience of life broadens and deepens. Verbalizing must never outrun real understanding based on experience; conversely, each new insight or idea presents a new problem of expression. Therefore the responsibility for training in the use of the English language is a joint and continuing responsibility of the school and of the college.[1]

Ideally, students should learn to write well because they want to write well—because writing well is important to them and they take pride in being able to command a prose style that is lucid and supple, faithful to the conceptions behind it, and mindful of the person or persons to whom it is addressed. Actually, this attitude may never develop in some college students, and it will be slow to develop in nearly all others. Our society affords too many illustrations not merely of the inexact and irresponsible use of language but of the rewards of power and wealth that such use often brings with it. Advertising provides the most glaring instances, but others can be found in editorial writing and in the utterances of many political figures, businessmen, and spokesmen for such groups as labor unions, physicians, and self-styled guardians of Americanism.

Members of a college faculty, therefore, whose business is to develop and train the minds of their students, should make it plain that they consider the ability to write clearly, correctly, and accurately a necessary part of a liberal education and as far as possible conduct their courses in a way that emphasizes the importance of using language responsibly. As the "Harvard Report" on general education said some years ago,

> This is not a question of tackling spelling or grammar considered as a routine quasi-mechanical skill, or of "good English" in

[1] *General Education in School and College*, Cambridge, Mass.: Harvard University, Press, 1952, p. 41.

any vaguely general sense. It is a question of giving practice and help in understanding and using the English which is the indispensable medium of their own teaching. A science teacher, for example, is not "taking over what the English class should have done" when he gives time and labor to this. Parroting apart, the language as used in a subject is in practice indistinguishable from the subject itself. In working on it he is doing his own work, not the English teacher's work.[2]

But unless a large majority of the faculty cooperates in the general endeavor to maintain standards of good writing throughout the college or university, many students will write with increasing carelessness the farther away they get from their freshman English courses. They are not intentionally being perverse; rather, since so few of them have gained a genuine conviction of the importance of good writing, they find it natural to give no more care to their writing than their teachers demand of them. They will be confirmed in their impression, formed during twelve years of pre-college schooling, that precise and accurate English is an exasperating dialect that one uses when writing for English teachers but rarely in other circumstances. (Witness the indignant outcries from students when a professor of economics or philosophy is bold enough to mark their papers down for poor writing: "But this isn't a freshman English course!")

The problem, then, is twofold: to determine what, if anything, can be done to persuade a majority of the faculty members of a college or university to accept their responsibility in requiring as much careful writing as possible from their students; and to discover what other pressures, if any, can be brought to bear on students so that they will continue trying to write as well as they can after they have completed the required freshman composition courses.

In keeping with the general procedure of the Dartmouth study—to make a close examination of student writing at one college, then develop a broader context by studying the problem less intensively at other colleges—a questionnaire was sent to all teachers of undergraduate courses at Dartmouth to find out what the attitudes and policies of the faculty are toward written work in their own courses.

[2] *General Education in a Free Society*, Cambridge, Mass.: Harvard University Press, 1945, p. 116.

The results of such a questionnaire, no matter how carefully it has been prepared, must usually be regarded with a certain skepticism, principally because there is seldom any tactful way to check on the validity of the replies or to be sure that they are being interpreted accurately. One teacher may report that he asks for, and gets, no less than 20,000 words of writing from each student each term—three times as much as most freshman English courses require—and the person tallying the answers must simply record the figure, trusting that the teacher's estimate represents fact, not wishful fancy. Another teacher may say that he refuses to tolerate "bad writing" and penalizes it severely. His views of the standards for judging the quality of student prose, and his conception of a severe penalty, may coincide with those of English teachers; but often his notion of good and bad writing may be largely restricted to writing that does or does not follow his own preferences on half a dozen matters of usage (*shall* and *will*, *due to* as a preposition, *like* as a conjunction), and his interpretation of a severe penalty may consist of no more than a hortatory note on the offending paper as a sign of displeasure, with the grade unaffected. Still another teacher who uses a great many machine-scored tests may feel a little diffident about revealing the full extent to which he uses them, especially when he is aware that the inquiry comes as part of an effort to promote more and better writing in other courses. When he fills out the questionnaire, he may therefore unconsciously tend to underestimate the amount of objective testing done in his courses and to magnify the amount of time given to essay testing.

The table on the next page summarizes some of the results of this questionnaire. Although one should keep in mind the limitations just mentioned, a few generalizations may be hazarded that are not without interest, for the results are probably not much different from those one might get from a similar questionnaire at other colleges.

1. Between a fourth and a fifth of the teachers who completed the questionnaire said that they require no papers in their courses. In some instances, no doubt, the nature of the subject matter minimizes the importance of such assignments—a course in principles of accounting, for example, or various courses in science or mathematics in which the written work consists mainly of formulas, equations, brief explanatory notes, and the like. But often teachers of courses in which one would expect occasional essays and investigative papers to be useful pointed

RESULTS OF QUESTIONNAIRE ON UNDERGRADUATE WRITING

	HUMANITIES * (117 QUESTIONNAIRES)		SOCIAL SCIENCES (128 QUESTIONNAIRES)		NATURAL SCIENCES (92 QUESTIONNAIRES)	
	N	%	N	%	N	%
Number of papers required:						
0	22	19	36	28	26	28
1–3	54	46	68	53	16	18
4–6	14	12	10	8	9	10
More than 6	13	11	5	4	27	29
No reply	14	12	9	7	14	15
Hours of essay testing:						
0	19	16	19	15	37	40
1–3	60	51	54	42	32	35
4–6	23	20	38	30	13	14
More than 6	1	1	3	2	2	2
No reply	14	12	14	11	8	9
Penalties for poor writing:						
Require rewriting	13	11	3	2	15	16
Mark defects	62	53	55	43	47	51
Reduce grade (but not fail)	54	46	41	32	32	35
Fail paper	30	26	17	13	1	1
Refer to clinic	22	19	22	17	2	2
No reply	39	33	60	50	39	42

* Excluding freshman English.

to the large size of their classes and said that they lack time to read and mark papers from so many students.

2. About half the teachers in the humanities and social sciences reported that they require between one and three papers each term. A relatively large number of teachers in the natural sciences said that they

require more than six papers a term, but this quantity is explained by the fact that the papers are laboratory reports, which as a rule must be submitted weekly. Usually these reports are not papers in the customary sense of connected prose compositions but rather a series of briefly reported observations or a combination of prose and mathematical or other formulas.

3. Roughly 40 per cent of the teachers in the natural sciences reported that they give no tests that require extended answers in prose. This seems mainly the result of the nature of the subject matter, which can be better tested by other means than essay questions. In the humanities and social sciences, teachers said they customarily require between one and three hours of essay testing.

4. About half the teachers in all three divisions said that they mark defects in the writing of their students. A little less than half the teachers in the humanities said they reduce the grade on a paper or test if the writing in it is bad; only a third of the teachers in the other two divisions reported their willingness to reduce a grade for this reason.

5. Only a fourth of the teachers in the humanities (most of them from the English department) said they will go so far in their disapproval of bad writing as to fail an ill-written paper for this reason alone. Thirteen per cent of the social science teachers said they will fail a paper that is badly written; 1 per cent of the science teachers said they will.

6. Few teachers in any of the three divisions seemed inclined to send students to a writing clinic (which was then in existence) for remedial help—an interpretation borne out by other evidence to be presented below.

In the hope of rounding out the picture presented by the questionnaire, a random sample of papers was studied from a variety of teachers and courses at Dartmouth, but the results were inconclusive. It was, in the first place, impossible to get a sample from any one course that would be comparable to the sample chosen from the freshman English classes, since no other regular academic course enrolls all students. Papers written by students in a course in sociology or geology or education could not be expected to be as representative of the writing of the student body as a whole. Other disadvantages were that many of the papers were too long to be analyzed with the necessary thoroughness; often the papers could not be spared long enough by the teachers to allow for analysis; and in some courses the only writing required was hour examinations, which, because they are written under pressure and not revised, cannot fairly be compared with papers written under less difficult circumstances.

The most that can be said on the basis of this limited investigation of writing in other courses is that the students whose papers were examined tended to write carefully if careful writing was demanded of them and to write negligently if standards were lax. Not surprisingly, there was wide variation in the intensiveness with which the writing itself was marked by teachers and in the degree to which the marks and criticisms agreed with standards generally used by English teachers when evaluating student prose. Such generalizations as these merely confirm what one already knows or would suspect about the state of writing at Dartmouth or indeed any other college.

A more fruitful line of inquiry proved to be an analysis of writing done in two quasi-academic programs that all Dartmouth students are obliged to participate in: the General Reading Program and the well-known Dartmouth Great Issues course. In the former, all freshmen and sophomores are obliged to select and read three books a year from prepared lists of books in the humanities, natural sciences, and social sciences and to write critical commentaries on them —a total of six books for each student in the two years. The commentaries must be at least 900 words long. In the Great Issues course, seniors attend lectures by some two dozen outside speakers during the year and take part in supplementary discussion meetings on the lectures; until the 1961–1962 school year, they also were required to write extensive journals (16,000 to 20,000 words during the year) containing their reactions to the lectures and to specified reading, and to submit a 3,000-word essay analyzing five different magazines of opinion.[3]

In neither of these programs is writing itself considered to be a principal object. Rather, it is strictly subordinate to other aims, as indeed it would be in any course except one in English composition. Yet both programs have made a conscious effort to enforce standards of good writing, both in principle and in practice. A Great Issues pamphlet giving directions for the preparation of the 3,000-

---

[3] In 1961–1962 the Great Issues journal was discontinued. At present the only writing done in the course is one research paper between 3,000 and 3,500 words long, which is read by the several Great Issues instructors (i.e., leaders of discussion sections).

word papers says that they "should meet a high standard of English prose." The standards for the journals are stated more specifically:

> Journals must be written in such style and form as may be expected of seniors at Dartmouth College. Any journal marred by numerous misspellings or careless grammar will be marked Unsatisfactory. . . . Experience shows that more journals are failed because of faulty grammar and spelling than because of inadequate content. The importance of correct and effective use of English cannot be overstressed.

The pamphlet on the General Reading Program, after discussing at length the required form and characteristics of the commentaries, says that "the commentary must measure up to college standards of literacy in spelling, punctuation, usage, and structure. These standards are the same as those of Freshman English. Papers failing to meet them will have to be rewritten."

The procedures and policies for grading the commentaries and journals must be mentioned because they have affected the attitude of students toward the writing that these two programs require. And the students' attitude toward this practice has naturally had a bearing on the value derived from it.

The Great Issues journals were graded by the three full-time instructors employed by the program and by the members of the Great Issues Steering Committee, which is composed of faculty members from various departments. All of the 3,000-word papers written in Great Issues were read and graded by a person employed part-time for this purpose alone. Both journals and papers were given one of three grades: "Distinction," "Credit," or "Unsatisfactory." The final grade in the course was—and still is—one of these three; but a course grade of "Distinction" converts to an A and to one term-course credit on the student's transcript, whereas a grade of "Credit" yields one term-course credit but no grade, and a grade of "Unsatisfactory" converts to an E, yields no course credit, and affects a student's point average as any other failing grade would.

The commentaries written by freshmen and sophomores in the General Reading Program are marked and graded by some twenty readers, college-educated women of the community who are selected primarily for their competence in particular fields of knowledge—mathematics, life science, social science, humanities, etc.—

within which a proportion of the books on the required reading list will fall.

The commentaries are graded "Superior," "Satisfactory," or "Unsatisfactory." No academic credit is given for participation in the program; but whenever a student has received two or more grades of "Superior" on commentaries, the fact is noted on his transcript. No notation is made on the transcript of grades of "Satisfactory" or "Unsatisfactory." A paper marked "Unsatisfactory" must, however, be rewritten; the student has the option of revising the paper in the ways indicated by the reader or reading a new book and reporting on it. If the new or rewritten commentary is also marked "Unsatisfactory," the author must receive special permission to submit a third paper. If a freshman has not submitted three satisfactory commentaries before the end of the first semester of his sophomore year, he is put on probation; if a sophomore has not completed six satisfactory commentaries by the end of the third term of his second year, he is suspended. Satisfactory completion of the General Reading requirement is prerequisite to enrollment as a junior.

A 10 per cent sample was selected from one set of journal entries in the Great Issues course, and another of the same size from the final set of commentaries handed in by sophomores in the General Reading Program. In both cases this meant sampling the work of about seventy men.[4] Photostats were made of these papers, and the copies were then carefully read and marked according to the standards imposed at the end of English 2. Ideally, it would have been best for purposes of comparing the sophomore and senior papers with those from English 1 and 2 if the freshman English staff had marked these papers; but since this was not possible, the director of the study and his assistant made the analysis, each marking all the papers independently, then resolving any disagreements that came to light. The errors were classified and recorded as in the freshman papers.

On page 109 is a table showing the results of the analysis both of the papers written by freshmen and of those written by sophomores and seniors. The figures look discouraging. In the papers studied,

---

[4] A 10 per cent sample was selected, rather than the 20 per cent sample chosen from English 1 and 2, because in analyzing the freshman papers it became evident that what was true of a 20 per cent sample was almost precisely true of a sample half that size.

sophomores made almost as many errors in their writing after a year and a half of college as freshmen do at the beginning of English 1 and more than freshmen make at the end of English 1. Seniors are worse than sophomores, having made more errors in their papers than freshmen do at the beginning of English 1. It is important to remember that this evidence does not necessarily mean that sophomores and seniors are writing this poorly in all their courses. That they should write so poorly for any academic purpose, however, is reprehensible. And the bad habits encouraged and strengthened by such writing become just that much harder to get rid of.

Rate of Errors per 1,000 Words of Writing: Freshmen, Sophomores, Seniors

Type of error	English 1			English 2			Soph.	Senior
	th. 1	th. 2	th. 3	th. 1	th. 2	th. 3		
A. Focus and structure	0.76	0.76	0.87	0.52	0.37	0.19	0.98	1.01
B. Material	3.53	3.24	2.75	2.30	1.87	1.97	2.75	4.89
C. Paragraphs	1.01	0.68	0.49	0.41	0.58	0.23	1.51	2.34
D. Sentences	4.84	3.57	2.30	3.27	2.97	2.56	5.99	8.24
E. Words	10.09	7.26	8.13	6.02	7.12	5.28	9.40	11.72
F. Grammar	1.17	0.82	0.76	0.56	0.43	0.36	0.79	1.56
G. Punctuation and Mechanics	4.79	3.55	3.37	3.16	4.22	3.47	5.01	7.99
H. Misspelling	3.62	2.59	2.33	2.28	3.01	2.16	3.21	4.22

The explanation of this performance appears to be simply carelessness. For example, as the first of the following two tables shows, there is no apparent correlation between high SAT Verbal scores and the kind of writing that sophomores and seniors did in the papers that were analyzed. Nor, as the second table shows, is there any predictable relation between what appears to be a good record in freshman English and the quality of the sophomore and senior papers as reflected by the grades assigned them in the analysis. Of particular interest are the paper grades of those sophomores who as freshmen were judged to be so competent in English composition that they were exempted from English 1.

GRADES GIVEN PAPERS BY SOPHOMORES AND SENIORS WITH HIGH SAT VERBAL SCORES

GRADE GIVEN PAPER	SOPHOMORES		SENIORS	
	SAT 600 & ABOVE	SAT 650 & ABOVE	SAT 600 & ABOVE	SAT 650 & ABOVE
A	2	2	1	1
B	6	4	4	2
C	11	5	8	3
D	12	6	7	3
E	9	5	7	3

GRADES GIVEN PAPERS BY SOPHOMORES AND SENIORS, IN RELATION TO RECORD IN FRESHMAN ENGLISH

GRADE GIVEN PAPER	SOPHOMORES			SENIORS	
	EXEMPT FR. ENG. 1 & 2	EXEMPT FR. ENG. 1	A OR B IN ENG. 2	EXEMPT FR. ENG. 1 & 2	A OR B IN ENG. 2
A	1	1	1		1
B		2	6	1	3
C		3	7	1	7
D	1	3	14		8
E		5	6		5

To test the possibility that the two readers who analyzed the papers and assigned these grades to them were unduly severe in their evaluations, the grades given the sophomore papers were compared with the grades given the same papers by the regularly employed readers for the General Reading Program. It was assumed that a grade of A is equivalent to "Superior," B, C, and D equivalent to "Satisfactory," and E equivalent to "Unsatisfactory." On this basis it was found that the two grades were the same on 64 per cent of the papers; 15 per cent of the papers were marked one grade lower by the readers for the Reading Program, and 21 per cent were marked one grade higher. The former discrepancy can be at least partly explained as the result of the readers' greater familiarity with the books that were being discussed and the fields of knowledge with which the books dealt; that is, they would be more aware of mistaken interpretations of the books and of erroneous notions about the general subject. The latter discrepancy is very probably due to the lesser familiarity of the readers with matters of rhetoric, usage, grammar, etc.; that is, the readers would generally not be as demanding in their assessment of a student's prose as someone whose principal concern is the teaching of writing and whose judgment of these matters should therefore be more expert.

In other words, though the two sets of grades were not identical, they were close enough to make it clear that the grades assigned the papers in the analysis were not excessively severe.

But if carelessness is at the root of these unhappy performances, what conditions permit or encourage such carelessness? Most central no doubt is that widespread feeling among students (and among some of their teachers) that good writing can be separated from good thinking, that "getting the general idea across" is enough for most purposes, and that one need not strive to write with clearness, correctness, and precision unless he is made to.

Other conditions contribute, too. In the General Reading Program the chief difficulty is that participation in the program is required for two years, yet no academic credit is given for the work. The theory behind this arrangement is admirable—that students of college age are mature enough to enjoy pursuing learning for its own sake and do not need to have a carrot dangled before their noses—or a stick brandished over their heads—in order to move in the direction that their intellectual development demands. In practice, the lack of credit has undoubtedly contributed to the slipshod work that many students (especially sophomores) have turned in. On the one hand, the lack of tangible reward in the form of official course credit has encouraged in many students an attitude of relative indifference—and sometimes hostility—toward the program. On the other, the inability of the readers to impose a penalty with a real sting in it has fostered carelessness and, apparently, among sophomores a measure of cynicism. The reader may mark a paper "Unsatisfactory" and thus oblige the student either to revise it or to read another book and write a new commentary. But an appreciable number of sophomores, who by their second year "know their way around," turn in a hastily and ill-written first draft, knowing that the reader will mark it "Unsatisfactory" but knowing also that the reader will not only offer them, without penalty, a second chance to turn in the paper but will conscientiously mark the errors and weaknesses in it, thus making revision a quick and painless job. Why, these students appear to ask themselves, should they go to all the trouble of writing and revising carefully in the first place, when they can do just as well by turning in a sloppy paper written in a fraction of the time and revise it easily and quickly by following expert free advice? It would be hard to find a more striking illustration of the aptness of the etymological meaning of *sophomore* ("a wise fool").

The following table shows the results of this attitude: In each of the three terms, 1961–1962, the sophomores wrote a significantly higher percentage of "Unsatisfactory" papers than the freshmen did. The table also shows two other things worth noticing. One is that

GRADES OF "SUPERIOR" AND "UNSATISFACTORY" GIVEN
IN GENERAL READING PROGRAM, 1961–1962

| | FALL, 1961 | | | | WINTER, 1962 | | | | SPRING, 1962 | | | |
| | FRESHMEN (804) | | SOPHS. (761) | | FRESHMEN (799) | | SOPHS. (741) | | FRESHMEN (787) | | SOPHS. (717) | |
	N	%	N	%	N	%	N	%	N	%	N	%
Sup.	36	4.5	38	5.0	50	6.2	30	4.0	48	6.1	34	4.7
Unsat.	102	12.7	136	17.9	72	9.0	87	11.7	59	7.5	93	13.0

the percentage of "Superior" grades given sophomores stays at the same dead level throughout the year; most of these grades are earned by the same men each time. The other is that there is a slight rise in the percentage of "Superior" grades given freshmen during the year and an encouraging decline in the percentage of "Unsatisfactory" grades given freshmen. Two explanations of the freshman grades come to mind: First, freshmen are less sophisticated in the ways of academic life than sophomores, more tractable, more likely to try to meet the requirements of the General Reading Program in good faith; and second, freshmen are either taking, or have very recently taken, one or more courses in freshman English, which appear to be exerting some influence on other writing done in the freshman year.

As for the quality of the writing displayed in Great Issues journals, it can be traced to some of the same causes that have produced so much careless writing in the sophomore papers. Among the most important are that participation in the course is compulsory, and that the amount of credit given does not seem to many students in proportion to the amount of time and work required. This situation has led to a certain amount of resistance toward the course and to a sometimes perfunctory attitude toward the writing assignments.

Another cause of poor writing in the journals—and perhaps the explanation of why the senior papers appear to be worse than the sophomore—is the system that was used for correcting the journals. The commentaries in the General Reading Program are read by people employed for the purpose and paid for their work; they are under explicit instructions from the director of the Program to mark the papers severely for errors in grammar and usage, as well as to take account of the quality of thought expressed in them and evidence that their authors have read and understood the books being written about. But many of the Great Issues journals were read by members of the general faculty who were serving on the Great Issues Steering Committee. Some of these teachers were meticulous in criticizing and marking the journals they read, taking account of the quality of the writing and allowing it to affect their evaluation of the journals. But, as always happens when a group of teachers whose main interest is not English are asked to mark papers for the quality of writing, not all were prepared or inclined to make this kind of criticism, with the result that standards among the readers varied widely. Some journals were returned to their authors carefully annotated and rigorously graded; others came back devoid of mark or comment except for a terse note on the grade sheet attached to each group of journal entries, and a grade that bore no apparent relation to the quality of the prose in which the entries were written.

These conditions tended to remove the writing of the journals from the plane of comparable academic tasks and to make it seem a less serious occupation; journal entries were something one could slap together in a couple of hours the night before they were due. A recognition of these circumstances appears to have been the principal reason why the journals were discontinued. Too few students were taking the writing of the journals seriously enough.

This analysis of the writing of sophomores and seniors in these two programs should not be interpreted as suggesting that only English teachers at Dartmouth cherish good writing or that Dartmouth students never write well except when they are laboring under the eye of an English teacher. But the analysis does suggest, and rather plainly, what will happen when standards are relaxed or when other circumstances persuade students that they need not exert themselves needlessly to write well. The analysis is, perhaps more than anything else, simply an undeluded commentary on the nature of American college students.

Until recently, one other device existed that, at least in theory, should have exerted a salutary college-wide influence on the writing of Dartmouth students. This was the writing clinic. Begun several years ago, the clinic offered free remedial help to any Dartmouth student who chose to come or who was sent there by one of his teachers. The service provided usually amounted to individual tutoring. Certain doubts finally arose, however, about the usefulness of the clinic, as a result of which an evaluation was made of it as part of the present study. The evaluation led to a recommendation that the clinic be discontinued. It was suspended on a trial basis and now seems unlikely to be revived. A review of the main points of the evaluation will be relevant here, since this kind of remedial provision is often suggested as the best way to enlist the cooperation of the entire faculty of a college or university in enforcing standards of good writing in their courses and to raise the quality of student prose in general to an acceptable level.

Shortly after it was begun, the clinic enjoyed a flurry of activity, mainly because of its novelty but also because the member of the English department in charge of it worked hard to solicit customers. When this person left the job, the clinic fell into less devoted hands, and business at once dropped off; only four students attended in the term following his departure. A new director took charge of it then, and business picked up once more; the attendance record was impressive enough to become an argument for continuing the clinic.

There were other arguments as well for keeping it on. One was that the existence of the clinic made it possible for teachers throughout the College (including readers for the Great Issues course and the General Reading Program) to insist on good writing from their students without themselves having to assume the responsibility for instructing them in the fundamentals of English composition. They merely had to refer offending students to the clinic for expert help. Another argument was that the clinic made it possible for the student of relatively low linguistic aptitude to get remedial help in English and so bring his writing skill more nearly into line with his general intellectual capacity. Finally, since attendance at the clinic was compulsory for students referred to it by the faculty, the mere threat of referral should have served to maintain writing standards throughout the College at a somewhat higher level than if the threat did not exist. (This last argument assumed, of course, that enough referrals would be made by the faculty so that students would realize there were teeth in the rule.)

The trouble with most of these arguments is that they were theoretical. In a better world they ought to have worked; in practice, at Dartmouth College, they did not work very well. The mere existence of the clinic, ironically enough, appeared to have the effect of confirming many teachers in other departments in their belief that good writing is solely the business of the English department, and that they themselves need assume no responsibility for helping to maintain acceptable standards of writing in their courses, except to send the worst offenders among their students to the clinic.

But judging from results, almost no students offended. During the last four terms that the clinic existed the faculty ignored it. In that period only six students were referred by the faculty—four from post-freshman courses in English, two from a course in government. In the same period of four terms only four students enrolled in the clinic on their own initiative. Nor did readers in the Great Issues course make any significant use of the clinic's services in the four-term period—this in spite of overwhelming evidence of much bad writing in the journals. In the two terms just after the new director took charge, twelve students from Great Issues were enrolled in the clinic, but the reason was that the director had asked the Great Issues Steering Committee to let him see the five most poorly written journals received by each member of the Committee. He then called the poorest or most careless writers in for a conference and persuaded twelve of them to enroll. In the two subsequent terms, only three students from Great Issues used the clinic.

The great majority of the students who attended the clinic in the four-term period came from the General Reading Program—84 per cent of the total. The explanation is simply that the director of the Program was an English teacher and therefore was seriously concerned to maintain high standards of composition in the Program. He had asked his readers to refer to the clinic any student whose commentary was marked "Unsatisfactory" because of poor writing. One might argue that evidence of this much use of the clinic should have justified its continued existence. The argument is not without merit. But when the English records of those men who attended the clinic were examined, it was discovered that 110 of them (80 per cent of the total of 139) had earned an average grade of C— or above in English 1 and 2. Eighty men (60 per cent) had earned grades in English 1 and 2 that averaged C+, C—. If these grades were an indication of demonstrated ability to write with a fair degree of competence, it seemed clear that the great majority of students referred to the clinic for poor writing were quite capable of remedying their own deficiencies without special help from the clinic. All that was needed was to convince them that they had to.

On the strength of this evaluation it was decided to drop the clinic. There seemed little possibility of getting the continuing cooperation of most of the faculty in referring poor writers to the clinic; and the evidence suggested that the great majority of Dartmouth students can write decent prose if they are convinced that it is important for them to do so. At colleges with less selective admission policies a greater need may exist for some kind of remedial service for poor writers beyond that offered in the freshman English courses. A clinic might be useful in such colleges if the right students could be induced to attend it. But, as will be mentioned later, the difficulty that the Dartmouth clinic encountered in getting the faculty to identify poor writers and require them to seek help is by no means unique.

At this point it will be useful to summarize the state of student writing at Dartmouth for the light it may throw on the comparable situation at other colleges. In spite of the prevailing emphasis on literature in the freshman English courses at Dartmouth, the supervised practice in writing in these courses does appear to produce visible improvement in the writing of most students, though the degree of improvement often is considerably less than one would like. Some students get (and deserve) grades of D or E, and some who get C—'s have only a precarious grasp on competence in composition. But by the end of their first year the majority either have demonstrated or seem on the way to attaining the skill in writing that is expected of educated adults. That is, they write this way in their freshman English courses, where their best efforts are regularly called for. They do not necessarily write this way in courses where the teachers take a more relaxed attitude toward excellence in written work. Many students backslide after freshman English when they are permitted to. Few have yet developed that sense of pride in their own writing that ensures that they will habitually write well without external pressures. It is true that the writing of students of this caliber, at Dartmouth and elsewhere, is seldom hopelessly bad even when it has been most carelessly done. Often it can hardly be said to be creditable either to its authors or to the college that is educating them; but even at its worst it lacks the unmistakable stamp of confirmed illiteracy that marks the efforts of many students in remedial courses. Dartmouth students, and their counterparts on other campuses, can write well enough if they are shown how, are given adequate practice, and are expected always to write to the best of their ability no matter what the course.

The Dartmouth faculty is probably more aware of the importance of clear and correct writing than are teachers at institutions that have a less humane tradition behind them than Dartmouth does. But even so, Dartmouth professors show a wide range of policies and attitudes toward student writing, many of which encourage habits that conflict with those that the English department is supposed to establish in the freshman year. In this respect the Dartmouth faculty is undoubtedly typical of American college and university faculties generally. The amount of writing, exclusive of tests, that is required of Dartmouth students varies greatly from one teacher to another, ranging from none at all to as much as sixty typed pages in a single term. But even when necessary allowances have been made for those courses in which it is not easy to assign the usual sort of papers, considerably less writing is asked for than should be if a constant pressure is to be maintained on students to write well throughout their undergraduate years. The amount of essay testing varies with the nature of the subject, the size of the class, and the convictions of the teacher. Probably not more than one or two hours per term of this kind of testing are required on the average; the figure may well be less.

The faculty in general is reluctant to be severe about marking and penalizing student writing when it is faulty. To some extent this attitude is understandable. Some teachers honestly do not feel qualified to do a thorough and competent job of marking papers for grammar, usage, and rhetoric. More important, reading papers in this way takes extra time, and teachers of physics or government or anthropology feel that they already have full-time jobs teaching their own subjects. Asking them to mark papers for the quality of the writing in them will seem to many teachers, whether rightly or wrongly, a gratuitous addition to an already full load, and they will refuse to accept the job.

But even when teachers of other subjects do mark errors in student writing, most are opposed to lowering the grade on the paper for this reason alone. Though they may agree that good writing is important, they are not sure it is *that* important. A professor of philosophy was heard to complain of the wretched prose that some of his juniors and seniors were turning in to him. The English teacher to whom this lament was addressed asked him, "But of course you are failing these papers, aren't you?" No, it appeared that, bad as the writing was, the students hardly deserved to be failed for having perpetrated it. "Then no doubt you lowered the grade, even though you didn't fail the papers?" Well, no, after all it wasn't an English course, and it was really not quite fair to reduce the grade "just for the writing when the ideas were all right."

Behind this teacher's attitude is the common notion that the English department should teach students to write when they are freshmen, and the ability should ever after stay with them, untarnished even when seldom used. But, as already pointed out, such an attitude is mistaken, since it is based on a misunderstanding of the writing process and of the problem of teaching writing. General intellectual development and the ability to verbalize new knowledge go hand in hand; inevitably, therefore, all teachers are to some extent teachers of English. An English course cannot permanently immunize a student to errors of thought and expression, any more than a course in ethics can ensure a lifetime of virtue. All teachers under whose influence a student comes should try, as far as they are able in the particular circumstances of the course, to enforce accuracy and clarity of expression, both oral and written, as a normal part of their responsibility to the student and to their own discipline. As a part of their responsibility to the society of educated men and women, they should also try to enforce reasonable conformity to those patterns of linguistic usage accepted by that society —in short, what we call correctness. The English teacher cannot do the job alone.

ATTEMPTS AT OTHER COLLEGES TO MAINTAIN STUDENT LITERACY

Backsliding after freshman English has been completed appears to be universal in American colleges and universities. The measures that Dartmouth College has tried in an effort to arrest the backsliding have already been described, but the size and nature of the difficulty can be seen even more clearly if some of the measures that have been tried on other campuses are examined. Unfortunately, they offer little ground for optimism. No one has so far discovered a way to keep students writing well in all their courses, nor does it seem at all likely that anyone will.

The devices that have been tried may be divided into two general categories: those that attempt in one way or another to coerce students into writing well; and those that attempt to persuade the faculty to help coerce students into writing well. Behind them all is a negative attitude, an unstated assumption that most students must be *forced* to try to write carefully and responsibly, that they lack the maturity or the perspicacity to recognize the importance to them of such writing and therefore cannot be relied upon to develop their own motivation. Probably everyone concerned with devising these measures or administering them is keenly aware of their fatal limitation, knowing well that they are mere palliatives and that the only solution is a general conviction among students that good writing and good thinking are inseparable and that both are characteristic of a liberally educated adult. But students are not likely to develop this conviction as long as their other teachers, in school and college, so often reveal that they themselves lack it.

By far the most common device that attempts to put direct pressure on students is the proficiency examination in composition. In the survey of writing programs at ninety-five colleges and universities, mentioned in an earlier chapter, this device was found being used at almost twice as many colleges and universities as any other. In its usual form it consists of an impromptu composition to be written in one or two hours on a choice of topics supplied either by the English department or, more often, by the committee that administers the examination. Sometimes the examination is required of all students at a certain point in their college career—most often either the junior year or the last term of the sophomore year. At some colleges, students who received grades of B or A in freshman English are exempted from the examination; at others those who got C or above are exempted. Often transfer students are obliged to take it, regardless of their freshman English record. The examinations are most often graded by members of the English department, which sometimes also administers the test; or they may be graded by members of an interdepartmental committee that has charge of the test. When the examination comes in the sophomore year, passing it is generally prerequisite to enrolling in upper-division courses; when it comes in the junior or senior years, it is likely to be a requirement for graduation.

Though proficiency examinations are widely given, almost no one appears to be satisfied with them. One complaint is that when all or most students are obliged to take such a test in an institution enrolling 5,000 or 10,000 students, the job of reading the papers becomes enormous, especially since borderline and failing papers usually must be read by at least two readers. A few universities have therefore rationalized the problem and gone over to machine-scored tests, usually an alternate version of the placement test that is given in the freshman year. The trouble with this plan is that students do not take this kind of test as seriously as they do the writing of an extended essay, so that the test loses much of its presumed value.

But the principal complaint is that although a proficiency examination may have some moral force, it is still just one more obstacle that a student can scramble over, then forget about once more. It does not exert that steady pressure on the student that is needed for genuine and lasting improvement. Probably it is not entirely without value, but no one has been heard to claim that it solves the problem that it deals with. A fairly exhaustive inquiry turned up only one school where the faculty appeared to be reasonably well satisfied with such an examination. The explanation lay in the fact that the test was new, having been given only once so far, and was being taken by only a part of the students enrolled in the arts and sciences division, so that the number of papers to be read was small.

The second most popular device used in an effort to raise the general level of student writing is the so-called writing "clinic" or "laboratory." This usually is no more than a kind of formalized tutoring service. Staffed mainly by graduate assistants or very junior instructors for a certain number of hours each week, a clinic offers free remedial service to students referred by members of the faculty for poor writing, to students who may have failed a proficiency examination, and to a handful of conscientious students who voluntarily attend because they think they need this kind of help.

There seems little question that this instruction is valuable for those students who take it seriously and are willing to learn. But the kind of student who is required to attend a writing clinic is usually not well disposed toward English or especially gifted in composition; often he is the marginal student who will not last the four years. Mainly because of the much diminished interest shown by the better colleges and universities in this kind of student in the last few years, writing clinics and laboratories are on the decline. They are likely still to survive where state laws require that state-supported colleges and universities admit all high school graduates; where large numbers of students transfer from junior colleges, where they earned credit for freshman English; or where, as at one of the Big Ten universities, a remedial English course has been abolished and a clinic now takes the place of the course, with the important difference that under the new arrangement attendance is voluntary.

Almost as common as the writing clinic is the practice of withholding the degrees of students who still give evidence of writing poorly when they are ready to graduate. Most often such evidence will consist of failure to have passed a proficiency examination within a certain time limit before the date of graduation, or to have neglected to remove whatever penalty was imposed because of failing the examination. Degrees may be withheld also when a student has failed to remove some sort of condition that was placed on one of his course grades because he wrote poorly in that course.

Imperiling a student's graduation because he writes poorly is a stringent measure and, within limits, it gets results. It thoroughly sobers a lazy or feather-brained student and sets him to work in an exemplary way. Unfortunately, though he may be told of the threat year after year to the very threshold of graduation, it seldom seems real to him until the last minute, so that his spurt of activity does not last long enough to do him much good. He runs to the clinic (if there is one) or hires a tutor or beseeches his almost-forgotten freshman English teacher and does his best to develop the necessary skill under what might be called forced draft. Probably most of the time he succeeds in finally getting over the hurdle. But if he does not, the officials of the college or university must be prepared to assume a flinty imperviousness to criticism from quarters that may often surprise them, and to resist all kinds of pressures to relax the rule and let "just this one student" get through. A university in the Midwest that had such a rule found itself under pressure from representatives of the armed services a few years ago when the degrees of several men were withheld because they still had not passed a proficiency examination which they could have taken (but did not) at any of five times in their last two years. These men had completed advanced ROTC and were headed for commissions after graduation; but until they graduated, they could not be commissioned. The university stood its ground, and the young men entered service as privates instead of second lieutenants. They later took the examination in absentia, passed it, and received their degrees.

The weakness of this practice of withholding degrees is that, like the proficiency examination, it does not exert a steady and continuing pressure on the student to write well. In theory it should, for the requirement is there staring at him for four years; but in practice, human nature being what it is, the requirement usually does not begin to affect the kind of student for whom it exists until late in the senior year. And by then it has become just another hurdle.

Some colleges have a policy of encouraging teachers in all subjects to attach some kind of condition to a course grade when a student has written poorly in that course. At a state university in the Southeast, a *cc* (composition condition) is placed after the course grade and no student can graduate as long as one of his grades is so stigmatized. The student removes a *cc* by attending a writing clinic and finally being certified by the clinic that he now writes creditably. Another state university urges its faculty to give a grade of "Incomplete" for bad writing; and if the course is one required for graduation, the presence of an "Incomplete" on the student's transcript effectively bars him from graduation until it has been removed. Here also the delinquent student must attend a writing clinic and pass an examination that in effect certifies that he has mended his ways.

Strictly enforced, either of these plans ought to get at least fairly good short-range results. Their fatal weakness is that, except for some English teachers and a handful of others (nearly always in the humanities), the faculty will rarely go to such extreme lengths to indicate their displeasure with the quality of a student's writing. At the first of the two universities mentioned above, the "cc" plan started out auspiciously, but now only twenty-five or thirty grades a year are so marked—in a university of some 9,000 students. At the other university, which has an enrollment of 10,000 undergraduates, a total of 57 students received an "Incomplete" for poor writing over a period of four full terms in 1960–1961. If one estimates that each of the 10,000 students took an average of five courses each term, the total number of course grades in four terms must have been between 150,000 and 200,000. Fifty-seven does not seem a very impressive fraction, especially when one discovers that the university is obliged by law to accept all high school graduates and that the public schools in this state are among the poorest in the nation. Not surprisingly, the great majority of the fifty-seven "Incompletes" were given to students enrolled in post-freshman courses in the English department.

At some colleges and universities an additional course in composition is required for students who have given evidence that they do not write up to the expected standard. Sometimes these are students who have failed a proficiency examination; sometimes they are upperclassmen who received D's in freshman English and are therefore still considered poor risks in composition; sometimes they are students identified by spot checks made of upper-division papers by a faculty committee.

Most frequently, these students are obliged either to take a non-credit remedial course at the freshman level or to repeat without credit the first semester of the regular freshman English course. A few schools require that an advanced course in expository writing be taken for credit. Either plan has the advantage of putting the student through a full course of ten or fifteen weeks and thus giving him both instruction and repeated practice in writing. The advanced course, however, is not likely to be very advanced when it is populated heavily with students who have got into trouble because of poor writing. Instead, it may easily become a junior-level remedial course. And when upperclassmen are sent back to a freshman English course which they must repeat without credit, they will almost inevitably form an indigestible lump in the class, making things difficult both for the freshmen who belong in the course and for the teacher in charge of it. These are not conclusive arguments against the practice of requiring an extra course for poor writers; but they must be reckoned as part of the price of such an arrangement.

A few universities have established faculty committees that periodically call for a set of papers or examinations from all post-freshman courses. These are spot-checked by the committee to identify poor writers, who must then take a proficiency test. Those who fail to pass the test may secure tutoring on their own initiative or, in extreme cases, may be required to take a noncredit course in composition. No student who has been identified by the committee as a poor writer can graduate until he has satisfied the committee's requirements.

The chief disadvantage of this plan is obvious: It imposes an enormous amount of work on the members of the committee in an institution of even moderate size—provided, of course, that the committee takes its duties seriously and reads enough papers often enough and carefully enough to be reasonably sure of sorting out the students that need attention.

Short of the sudden conversion of all teachers to the belief that good writing is really important, perhaps the most satisfactory device to exert continuing pressure on students to write well after the freshman year is to schedule a series of required courses in which good writing is regularly expected. Such a plan is hard to put in execution because of the many demands on the class time of college students, but it can be carried out with varying degrees of thoroughness. Several universities require more than one year of English of most students. The most common pattern calls for a year of composition, followed by a year of literature; in the latter, considerable writing is asked for, and it is judged by standards at least as rigorous as those in the composition course. One university varies the pattern, requiring one semester of composition in the first half of the freshman year, then a whole year of literature, then a second semester of composition in the second half of the sophomore year. A state college in the Northwest has spread the three terms of the freshman communications course over three years, one term each year from freshman through junior years. The last two courses have been made progressively more difficult, so that they are not merely freshman courses moved to later years but advanced courses suited to the greater maturity of the students taking them. Probably the most impressive plan is that at a distinguished engineering school. A year's course in English is required in both the freshman and sophomore years; in the junior year students are required to elect one of several courses in literature; and in the senior year all are obliged to take a humanities course. In all the courses in this sequence considerable writing is required, and it is judged for quality.

The remaining devices that will be mentioned are those that attempt, always gently and tactfully, to exert some degree of pressure on faculty members to demand good writing of their students or at least to cooperate in a general effort to raise the standard of student prose to a point where it will not disgrace its authors and the institution that is giving them an education. For reasons that have already been mentioned, however, such appeals never meet with much success.

The most frequently used device to secure the cooperation of the faculty is a policy of referring poor writers to some other agency for remedial instruction in English. Teachers of other subjects are urged to take this step so that they can feel satisfied in the knowledge that they are helping to uphold standards of good writing, yet need not take on themselves the burden of tutoring students in English grammar and usage. Erring students are sometimes sent to a writing clinic; sometimes they are made to report to the English department where they are arbitrarily turned over to whichever of several instructors happens to be available; sometimes they are advised to enroll in a remedial course; and at a few colleges they are simply directed to a tutor whom they must pay by the hour.

But experience has abundantly shown that most teachers are reluctant to refer as many students as they should—or even to refer any students at all. At an Eastern university where a referral policy has been in force, the dean of the college of arts and sciences not long ago sent out the following notice to the faculty of his division:

> The Committee on Divisional Examinations in the Humanities has reported a shocking situation. Twenty-four out of the 337 papers written by the senior class last May were found by each of the two readers to be below minimum standards of literacy.
>
> This means that approximately seven per cent of the senior class has been awarded degrees by the faculty without being able to write a satisfactory paper of moderate length. It is hardly conceivable that these students have done satisfactory written work for three years and then on this one occasion done unsatisfactory work.
>
> Bear in mind that not one of this seven per cent could have registered as a sophomore without having passed English 101–102. Obviously, as sophomores, they *were* able to write themes and examinations which met, at the very least, satisfactory standards.
>
> What has happened? The conclusion seems inescapable that the faculty has not been taking proper advantage of reporting to the English Department papers which do not meet satisfactory standards of literacy. For example, this last year only *four* faculty members reported a total of ten students out of a possible 2,335 students. Yet seven per cent of the senior class failed to meet minimum standards of literacy in an examination of fundamental importance.

Because of this reluctance of faculty members to single out poor writers and require them to seek help, several plans have been developed to make referral as easy and painless for the teacher as possible. One is a separate column printed on the final grade sheet for each course; in this column the teacher may simply place a check beside the name of any student whose writing he feels has been below standard during the course. Occasionally a single check will cause a student to be referred to a writing clinic, but more commonly the faculty has hesitated to make the rule so severe. Usually it takes two such checks to require a student to report for remedial help. The results are about what one would expect: few students receive two checks. For example, at one large state university where this system is in force, 285 students received one check each in a four-term period, but only 3 students received two checks and were forced to attend the clinic. All 285 were, however, sent polite notes by the English department inviting them to visit the writing clinic for a conference on their writing and for further help if they wished it. Most ignored the invitation. Forty did eventually show up, but nearly all of them came just the one time and then were seen no more. It is typical that more than half of the 285 who received one check had one of twelve teachers to thank for this attention; the teachers were all from the English department or one of the other humanities departments. The great majority of the faculty has continued to ignore the column on the grade sheet.

Another plan has been tried at a number of large universities in the Midwest. Quantities of gummed slips are printed reading something like this:

THE WRITING IN THIS PAPER IS UNACCEPTABLE

(　　) Your writing reveals many errors, probably due to carelessness. In the future, please edit your papers carefully before submitting them.

(　　) Your writing is so poor that your grade has been affected. You need to plan before you write, choose words more precisely, and edit with care.

(　　) Some of the writing errors in this paper are serious enough to require your immediate attention. Take this paper to the Writing Clinic, 314 Humanities Building, for assistance. These errors should not reappear in future papers.

(　　) Please correct the errors marked in this paper and return it to me within a week.

Pads of these slips are given out at the beginning of each year to every teacher on the faculty, together with a statement from the president or various deans urging all teachers to recognize the importance of good writing and to use these slips, simply attaching one to an offending paper and checking the proper comment. The plan seldom lasts more than two years. It starts out in a brisk flurry of gummed slips, with some teachers asking for additional pads before the first month is out. But the novelty soon wears off, and the slips are seen no more and never asked for again. At one university where the highest hopes were held for the scheme, no more than a dozen and a half students in the last year have reported for help with papers to which a gummed slip had been attached—this in a student body so large that undergraduates in the arts and sciences college alone number 6,500.

Another scheme that has been tried in an effort to persuade all teachers to take more interest in the quality of their students' writing is to establish a fairly large committee representing all academic divisions of the college or university. The theory behind this plan is the desire to give a representative group a direct stake in good student English, in the hope that they will proselytize among their own colleagues and do more good than the English department can, since it is always suspected either of trying to shirk its responsibilities or (somewhat contradictorily) of trying to enlarge its empire. Given such names as the "Committee on Student English," the "Committee on Prose Improvement," or the "Student Literacy Committee," these groups often have charge of the proficiency examination in composition, administering it and occasionally helping to grade the papers. At one large state college, such a committee issues an appeal every fall to the faculty to assign as much writing in their courses as possible and to lower grades for poor writing. At another college a committee has prepared for the faculty several pages containing uniform manuscript instructions and a list of grading standards with examples. At another a sample paper has been reproduced showing typical correction symbols and abbreviations for the guidance of teachers who are willing to mark errors in grammar, usage, and rhetoric in their students' writing. At this same college the committee has persuaded the college administration to buy a copy of a standard freshman handbook of grammar and usage for every office on the campus.

Probably all of these measures help; but probably none of them helps very much. Visits to several of the campuses where such measures have been undertaken revealed neither satisfaction with results nor confidence that the results would greatly improve. The blunt truth is that few faculty members outside the humanities really believe that good writing (correct, accurate, clear writing) is important. Some of them will voice pious acceptance of the principle but quail at putting it into practice. Others will believe that they are insisting on good writing when they are only insisting on writing that is superficially correct. Without turning a hair they will swallow cacophonous wording, disorganized paragraphs, and strings of eight or ten consecutive prepositional phrases, but they will strangle on a supposed misuse of "shall" or "will." Still others, it must be suspected, simply do not know good writing when they see it. Because of defects in their undergraduate and graduate training (for which, to be sure, they can scarcely be held responsible) and because of the particular jargon habitual to their own discipline, a simple, direct statement is often suspect to them: if it can be so easily understood, it cannot be saying anything important. Consider the following passages:

> The data, in general, suggest that neither similarity nor complementarity of needs appears to be particularly meaningful in the determination of adolescent friendships beyond the suggested importance of similarity in a case where an extreme difference in friendship choices exists. However, both of these need patterns are internally consistent phenomena and perhaps are related to other factors. Similarities in perceptual and cognitive phenomena appear to be promising leads for future research in this area.

> In conformity with the preceding point, if all the interacting parties (in marriage, in minority-majority groups, in different occupational, religious, political, economic, racial, ethnic, and other interacting groups and persons) view the given overtly similar (or dissimilar) traits: A, B, C, D, N (physical, biological, mental, socio-cultural) as negligible values or as no values at all, as comprising even no similarity (or dissimilarity), such overt similarities-dissimilarities are innocuous in the generation of either solidarity or antagonism.[5]

[5] The first of these passages is taken from an abstract of a doctoral dissertation in education. The second, which I first saw quoted in Robert Waddell's *Grammar and Style*, New York: William Sloane Associates, 1951, comes from P. A. Sorokin's *Society, Culture, and Personality*, New York: Harper & Row, Publishers, 1947.

If a teacher sees nothing wrong with such clotted prose as this—
or even if he tolerates it with no rise in blood pressure—how can
he be expected to recognize and value good writing and to insist
on good writing by his students? [6]

Though one comes to the conclusion reluctantly, it seems inescapable that short of trying to remake not only American education
from the kindergarten through the graduate school but a great part
of American society as well, no genuine cure is possible for the
careless, inexact, jargon-ridden language that a great many American
college students habitually use in their written work without
effective rebuke. But though a real cure seems out of the question,
it would be a great error for people whose business is education and
who recognize the crucial importance of using language responsibly
to sit idly by and do nothing to arrest tendencies that they know
to be, in the strictest sense, anti-intellectual. Though one can
only propose palliatives, they should still be proposed. Any gain
at all is worthwhile.

[6] It is worth pointing out that both of these selections are written in
correct English. The periods and commas are all in the right places, the words
are correctly spelled, the grammar is unexceptionable. The selections comprise a powerful demonstration that it takes more than correctness to make
writing good.

Chapter 5

Recommendations

RECOMMENDATIONS FOR FRESHMAN ENGLISH

The recommendations that follow are tempered by a lively appreciation of how fruitless it is to dogmatize about teaching composition: the need to read this or that kind of material, the importance of making students write on this or that kind of subject, the superiority of such-and-such a method of marking papers. There are many ways to teach composition, and nearly all appear to succeed from time to time.

But although these recommendations are offered in the knowledge that they are not the only possible answers to the many questions that composition teaching raises, they are not offered diffidently. They are defensible answers, if not infallible ones.

Administration

1. *Class size and teaching load.* If composition is to be well taught, classes must be small, and the number of classes assigned to any one teacher must be carefully limited. Ideally it might be best to teach writing—or any other subject—on an individual tutorial basis, but practically one must settle for a good deal less. Any specific limit that might be set is arbitrary, though perhaps the existing policy at Dartmouth (twenty students per class, two 4-hour classes per instructor) is as close to the ideal as most institutions can hope to approach and closer than many can aspire to. In the other direction, anyone who has ever tried to teach what is often regarded as a standard full load of freshman composition—four

3-hour classes of twenty-five to thirty students each—knows that this is much too heavy a schedule to allow for good teaching. It is too much of the same sort of thing, and it means too heavy a burden of paper work. The teacher should have enough time and energy to plan his assignments with care, prepare his class meetings, read assigned papers promptly and attentively and mark them thoroughly, and schedule conferences with students in need of special help. No teacher should be given more than three—better, two—classes of composition in any one term, though he might be assigned one or two classes of something else to fill out his schedule; and no composition class should enroll more than twenty-five students—better, twenty.

2. *Exemption from freshman composition.* To make no provision at all for exempting unusually able students from freshman composition is both unreasonable and unrealistic. No matter how high an opinion one may have of the value of a particular composition course, it is going too far to insist that the course is indispensable to the intellectual development of every student who enrolls at the college. Most freshman classes contain a few students who are at least as bright as their teachers and who are already able, no matter how they may have learned, to think systematically and clearly and to express their ideas with some distinction. An English department may set up a special course in the freshman year offering advanced work to these students, or it may simply let them bypass the freshman year and hasten them on to sophomore or upper-division courses.

The proportion of students for whom these provisions are made should be very small; they should be the cream of the cream. Granting wholesale exemptions from the freshman composition course usually betrays an impoverished notion of its purpose and possibilities. A course in English composition that deserves a place in an institution of higher education ought to offer more than narrowly utilitarian training in how to achieve linguistic respectability. Correctness should be one of the aims but not the only or even the chief aim. The course should endeavor instead to discipline the thought and written expression of the student through a study of the principles of rhetoric and logic and through practice in applying those principles; and generally it should also offer him the opportunity to study language and literature for their intrinsic interest and worth. From such a course as this only the exceptional student should be exempted.

3. *The freshman composition course taught by all ranks of teachers.* No matter how large the university or how many advanced-degree candidates it has who need subsidizing, no English department should use only graduate students and junior instructors to teach the freshman composition course. All the members of the department should teach a section of the course occasionally—not just honor sections populated by bright students but average sections as well. If possible, this assignment should be made on a regular schedule such as once every year or every two years. The schedule should be arranged so that in any term several ranking members of the department are teaching in the freshman program. Such a policy has the effect of enhancing the status of the freshman English course. And it also serves to restore the perspective of senior professors, who have a way of forgetting what typical freshmen are like and of overlooking the fact that poorly taught freshman courses eventually mean poorly prepared juniors and seniors in their own classes. If the freshman course is genuinely of college caliber—as it can and should be in reputable four-year institutions—teaching it need not be thought demeaning for any member of the English department, no matter how exalted his rank.

Teaching

4. *Planning assignments in composition.* All teachers of composition should recognize that planning an assignment in writing is one of the most important aspects of teaching composition, and it should accordingly receive their closest attention. An offhand assignment or one poorly thought through places every student under a needless handicap and guarantees that a sizable proportion of the papers will be defective. The teacher himself is then inconvenienced by the necessity of having to mark and explain all the defects, a time-consuming and often frustrating task. He should save himself (and his students) trouble by anticipating it, thinking through the assignment before he gives it, deciding what the assignment is intended to teach the students and what problems it presents, alerting the students to these problems but leaving it to them to work out their own solutions.

Most assignments in writing should be carefully planned to *teach* the student something specific, rather than be mere unfocused exercises or a mechanical fulfilling of a requirement that there be so many themes in a course. An assignment based on a literary work being studied ought to be so planned that the work or some aspect of it will be illuminated for the student as he organizes his thoughts and puts them on paper. But it should also be planned to teach him something specific about writing—about the uses of expanded definition, for example, or about the importance of establishing and maintaining a consistent point of view, or about inductive or deductive patterns of arrangement.

5. *Kind of writing to be assigned.* A college English department should agree on a policy governing the kind of writing to be assigned students in the required freshman composition courses, one that all members of the staff can subscribe to and will consent to abide by. In particular, the policy should specify the relation of the writing to assigned reading, and the predominant type of writing to be required. A possible policy for the basic course, the one in which the most direct effort is made to teach writing, would be an agreement that all but two or three papers should be based directly on the reading done in the course and should be expository in nature, usually papers of analysis or criticism. The remaining two papers could be assigned according to the individual teacher's preferences and at such times as best suited his purposes. They might, for example, be papers based on personal experience or observation and come as the first written assignments in the course; or one might be deferred and introduced later to provide some variety in the writing assignments. It is important to have a definite policy on kind of writing in the later course or courses of the sequence also, so that each course can be assumed to be providing approximately the same kind of training in all sections.

6. *Marking of student papers.* An English department should establish the policy that instructors consistently try to identify errors and weaknesses in student writing with as much precision as possible. The practice of using all-purpose symbols or abbreviations (*K, awk, ?*) to indicate dissatisfaction with a word or passage should usually be avoided. So should excessive rewriting or editing of defective passages, a practice that may set the passage straight but that often leaves the student uncertain of the specific principle he has violated. Handbook rule numbers have the virtue of being

specific, but teachers should not rely on them alone to indicate criticisms of student papers; the limitations of these symbols are first, that they are entirely impersonal, and second, that they necessarily signify negative criticism. They should be supplemented with comments referring both to particular passages and to the entire paper. Such comments are most helpful when they are specific, pointed, and constructive.

7. *Agreement on standards for judging student papers.* Even though an English department already agrees reasonably well on standards for judging individual papers in the freshman English courses, it should continue to explore all possible measures to secure even closer agreement. One such measure is to schedule theme-grading meetings—at least one each term, and preferably two in the autumn term when new instructors must become acquainted with the standards and policies of the department. It is highly desirable that these meetings be attended not just by the youngest and newest members of the staff but by senior members as well. Unless such meetings have the benefit of the mature judgment of senior staff members, they can accomplish only a part of their purpose. And the benefit works both ways: even the most experienced teacher can profit from such a meeting if only to reassure himself that his grading standards are not out of line with those of a majority of his colleagues.

A second device is to duplicate a student paper once or twice a year—preferably one of middle quality—and ask each staff member (or, in big departments, ten or a dozen teachers) to mark and grade it in keeping with his usual practice; then reproduce all the papers with the marks, comments, and grades that have been placed on them and distribute them as a small pamphlet for study and discussion by the staff. (The names of teachers who corrected particular papers need not be given.) This device is especially helpful to familiarize new staff members with departmental standards. And, if these members are not yet widely experienced in teaching composition, it is a good way to demonstrate methods of marking and criticizing papers and to alert these teachers to the need for taking account not only of mechanical matters but of such highly important though less obvious aspects of a paper as paragraph structure, transition, tone, organization, reader awareness, etc. The device is also a means of getting into the open those numerous disagreements about details of usage, diction, and similar matters, to which English teachers of all degrees of expertness are so prone. Once in the open, these matters can be rationally discussed, with the object of reducing the amount of disagreement.

A third and often-used measure that can help considerably to clarify criteria for papers at the various grade levels and to reduce wide variation in grading is to assign a departmental committee the task of selecting one student paper that is clearly of A quality, one of B quality, and so on through the full range of grades. These can be marked in a way satisfactory to the entire staff, then reproduced as a part of the theme instructions for new freshmen, who also benefit from this concrete illustration of the standards by which their papers will be judged in freshman English. Many departments that have prepared such pamphlets have found them a good means of informing high school English teachers of the kind and quality of work expected of college freshmen.

8. *Policy on misspelling and other gross errors.* A college English department should adopt a clear-cut and severe rule with respect to misspelling in student compositions. When students write outside of class where they have all the time they need to consult a dictionary and to proofread their papers, there is no excuse for misspelling. When they write impromptu papers and have less time for proofreading, the rule might be tempered a little at first. But before the term is far advanced, they should be expected to budget their time on impromptus so that they are able to proofread and to look up words they are unsure of; then they should be held to the same standard on these papers as on those written outside of class. The sooner a student is persuaded of the enormous social importance of conventional spelling, the sooner he will take pains to eliminate misspellings from his work—and the sooner, perhaps, he will gain a secure mastery over the spelling of the words he most often uses. The departmental rule should therefore be stringent, perhaps a failing grade for a three-page paper containing three or more separate misspellings. The rule might begin to apply with the third paper of the term, after students have been clearly and repeatedly warned.

It would not be a bad idea, in fact, to formulate a "blacklist" of gross errors in the mechanics of writing and to give the list to students at the beginning of the term, warning them that after a certain point in the term errors of these kinds will be severely penalized in their papers.[1] A departmental committee might be given the job of defining what the staff agrees to regard as a "gross" error in these matters. Though no attempt should be made to prepare a complete list (endless argument would result), representative errors ought to be identified. A guiding principle might be that no error should be considered a *gross* error if the opinion of competent language scholars is divided about it.[2] For example, "reason is because," "due to" as a preposition, most uses of "shall" and "will," "different than" are disputed usages. They may all be judged errors in particular contexts, but the fact that learned judges are not unanimous in regarding them as errors would exclude them from a list of *gross* errors. On the other hand, the list might include most errors of subject-verb agreement (but not such constructions as "a number of players were caught in the storm"), most errors in pronoun-antecedent agreement (but not "everyone in the audience got to their feet and faced the President's box"), most sentence fragments (but not responses, exclamations, or such locutions as "but to begin" and "now to the next question"), punctuation errors that cause misreading, as in "she arrived late for her car had broken down" (but not the omission of a serial comma before "and").

9. *Revision of papers.* Students should be required to revise all papers and return them to the instructor. A student who merely has his errors pointed out to him but who is not asked to correct them will generally be slower to eliminate the errors from future papers than the student who is made to correct his mistakes at the time he commits them. To encourage revision, teachers might announce that they consider satisfactory revision a part of the assignment and that the grade for a paper will not be recorded until the

---

[1] Such a rule was in force at Dartmouth until recently and may soon be restored. It read: "In a theme of average length—500 words—more than three elementary errors in grammar, punctuation, and spelling will fail a theme. For longer themes, the allowance of elementary errors is increased proportionately. This rule will remain in force throughout the freshman year." The rule was applied beginning with the fourth paper of English 1.

[2] This principle has been used at Fresno State College, where a no-nonsense attitude toward gross errors as defined here has been applied in freshman English with remarkable success in spite of the fact that Fresno State students are an average rather than highly selected group.

paper has come back revised. Though it adds to their labors, teachers should check revisions carefully to be sure that the student has corrected the error and not simply guessed wrong again.

10. *Final grades in freshman English courses.* In a required course taught in many sections by many different teachers, every effort should be made to maintain as close an agreement as possible on standards for reckoning course grades. Exhortation may help, but it seldom proves to be enough by itself. Other measures should also be tried to help individual staff members assess their own grading policies in the light of those of their colleagues. For example, at the end of each term the person in charge of the freshman English courses might prepare grade statistics for each teacher who has taught a section of freshman English in that term. These statistics should not be identified by teacher, but the copy sent each teacher should have the appropriate figures checked so he can know which ones refer to his own class. The quality of particular sections of these courses can vary considerably according to chance; but if a teacher discovers that his grades are substantially higher or lower than the average, term after term, he should begin to question his own standards.

Curriculum

11. *Elementary instruction in grammar, usage, and mechanics.* It is time that the English departments of reputable four-year colleges and universities announce that elementary instruction in the details of correct grammar, usage, and mechanics is not a proper activity for college classrooms. (A considerable number have already done so.) Class time should not be given to the discussion of these matters but should be reserved for instruction in material of college level. Such elementary errors should be marked when they appear in a student's writing and the student should be made to correct them in revision, but any instruction in them should be managed in personal conferences or simply by recommending that the student read certain sections of the handbook and so instruct himself. It is hard to believe that students who are capable of learning physics and French, college algebra and economics, are not capable of studying a handbook by themselves to learn the rules for forming the possessive case or the correct preposition to use with "different."

Where entrance requirements are low and substantial numbers of ill-qualified students must be admitted, a more formal arrangement for remedial instruction may be necessary. But it ought not to be considered a part of the English department's regular academic offerings even though it may be given without credit. Instead, it should be under the auspices of the extension division or should be an independent noncollegiate program with its own staff like the "English A" program at the University of California. The student who needs this work ought to be expected to pay a special fee for it; it should not be regarded as a normal obligation of an institution of higher education and included in the regular tuition fee.

12. *Class instruction in rhetoric.* If a principal aim of the required freshman English courses is to teach students to improve their ability to write expository prose, some provision should be made in these courses for explicit instruction in those principles of rhetoric that are especially pertinent to exposition. Instruction in the principles of rhetoric should not mean studying the so-called "Four Forms of Discourse," or Barrett Wendell's trinity of Unity, Coherence, and Emphasis, or the nine—or nineteen—ways to develop expository paragraphs. This kind of rhetorical instruction is both sterile and stupefying, as several generations of teachers and students have feelingly testified. What is recommended here is a systematic attempt to help students become actively aware of what goes on inside good expository prose so they may come to know a little more about the nature of the tools they themselves are using and thus perhaps learn to use them more intelligently. Only a few of the countless handbooks of rhetorical theory now on the market are worth considering as textbooks to guide this kind of study; but until more and better rhetorical handbooks are ready, profitable instruction can be given without them. A well-read teacher accustomed to making close analyses of poems and plays and novels can also illuminate expository prose by the same sort of analysis, if he turns his mind to the job. In other words, by analyzing expository selections chosen from the work of good writers, the teacher could guide students to an understanding of such matters as the importance of tone and how it is established, the principal patterns of organization and how choice of one or the other is determined by purpose, subject, and expected readers, the more important means of effecting transitions, how and why practicing writers actually

paragraph their prose (not the same thing as the paragraph theory
in most handbooks), the effects of parallel structure or looseness
or periodicity in sentences, the range and nature of a writer's
vocabulary and its relevance to what he is saying and how and why
he is saying it. Students should learn to make such analyses for
themselves, as well as to apply to their own composition the principles they derive from such analysis.

13. *Class instruction in the logic of exposition.* Like the principles
of rhetoric, a few of the principles of logic ought to be made known
to the student if he is to become a better writer of expository prose.
Though few English teachers are—or should be expected to be—
trained logicians, they and all other teachers teach some of the
elements of logic informally whenever they insist on clear thinking
in recitation or writing. It should be helpful to student and teacher
alike, in a course dealing with expository writing, to identify a
few of these principles of clear thinking so they become a conscious part of the student's equipment for analyzing the writing
and speaking of others and for guiding his own practice. Considering the restrictions imposed by time and by the formal training of
the teachers, the amount of this material to be included would have
to be severely limited. Though one might wish for more, it would
still be worthwhile to present no more than the principles of definition, the nature of evidence, and the main outlines of inductive
and deductive reasoning, taking care not to allow the discussion of
such devices of logic as the syllogism to become overcomplicated.

14. *Class instruction in language.* Ideally, a freshman English
program ought to contain a serious introduction to the study of
language, with special attention to English. This kind of instruction
has already entered many of the better high schools, and it is safe
to predict that in five years' time the nation's colleges and universities will be getting an appreciable number of freshmen who have
had the benefit of such study.[3]

---

[3] Perhaps the greatest impetus to this study has been given by the Commission on English of the College Entrance Examination Board. One of the most
important decisions of recent years affecting the teaching of English in the
lower schools may well prove to be that of the Commission when it selected
W. Nelson Francis of Brown University to lead the group in the summer of
1961 at Ann Arbor, Michigan, that planned a course in language. This was
given to 900 high school English teachers in the summer of 1962 on twenty
university campuses. Since Francis is a leading structural linguist, the partici-

Ironically, though the responsible study of the English language might be thought to be as much a part of the English teacher's professional obligation as the study of English and American literature, few college English teachers today are prepared to teach even the elements of an intellectually respectable view of the English language. Increasingly, English teachers are coming to realize this deficiency in their training and are setting out to remedy it by independent study or by attendance at summer school, though so far high school teachers seem more alert to the need than college teachers.

Meanwhile, desirable as it would be to incorporate in freshman English courses a major unit on language, and especially the English language, such a recommendation would at the present moment be unrealistic. Because of the long-established pattern of undergraduate and graduate curricula for future English teachers, few of the people who now teach freshman English are qualified to present this material. Most of them could of course pick up a book on structural linguistics and manage to keep a jump or two ahead of most of their students most of the time, but this obviously would not be good teaching. The teacher should know more about the subject than is in the textbook he asks his class to read.

Two steps should, however, be taken that would help to place most English departments in a stronger position with regard to language study than they now occupy and that would begin to head them in the direction they may eventually be obliged to move in when increasing numbers of freshmen come to college having been introduced in the lower schools to a responsible and up-to-date study of language. The first step would be to try out a limited

---

pating universities sent representatives to the institutes who were well informed about recent developments in language study, and most of whom were already committed to either structural or transformational linguistics. Nine hundred influential high school teachers were given a course in language that introduced them to linguistics, and they are already passing some of this knowledge along to their students. If federally supported institutes for English teachers become available under the National Defense Education Act, the Commission's institutes will serve as prototypes, thus guaranteeing an introduction to this kind of language study to many more teachers. With such interest developing, and with several good high school textbooks on linguistics already on the market, the study of language in the lower schools seems certain to be revolutionized in the next few years.

amount of material on language experimentally in a few selected sections of freshman English that have been assigned to teachers interested enough in this subject matter to be willing to prepare it in advance, as they would the content of any other new course. Depending on the time available, these sections might study one or more of a variety of aspects of language, such as the nature of language, the background of English, the principles of English structure, linguistic geography, lexicography, the bases of correctness in English, possibly something on American dialects. All these topics should be presented as humane knowledge, worth studying for its intrinsic interest and value; it is quite as important to establish the legitimacy of this point of view toward language study as it is to give students a grasp of any one of the topics themselves.

A second step would be for English departments to modernize their upper-division courses in language if these are already offered or to introduce up-to-date courses in language if none are now in the curriculum. The situation that now exists was made evident by a 1960 survey conducted by the National Council of Teachers of English. The survey revealed that among 374 liberal arts colleges and universities (about a fourth of the four-year institutions in the country), 42 per cent offered no course in history of the English language and 72 per cent offered no course in modern English grammar. In regard to the latter course, even this figure looked better than it was, for not all the departments in the 28 per cent that reported they were offering this course were construing "modern" in the same way; the textbooks that were being used in many of these courses present the outmoded Latin-based grammar that has long lacked scholarly respectability. At the time of the survey, probably no more than 15 per cent of the colleges were offering an up-to-date course in the study of English grammar.[4]

Courses that should be offered should include at a minimum the two already mentioned, as well as a more elementary course that would touch more lightly on half a dozen fields of language study and serve as a general introduction. The course in modern English grammar certainly should take account of the work of the structural linguists, as well as older systems such as those of Jespersen and the recent work of such scholars as Chomsky and Lees.

15. *Class instruction in literature.* This report has expressed some

[4] *The National Interest and the Teaching of English*, pp. 67–69.

reservations about the use of imaginative literature in a course that is supposed mainly to teach composition, but it has not intended to suggest any hostility toward the teaching of literature. Quite the contrary. In any institution that professes to offer a liberal education, the English department has an inescapable obligation to help every student gain a familiarity with and appreciation of some of the literary masterpieces of the English language. The teaching of composition and the teaching of literature are, or readily can be, closely related, as mentioned before; the question is only one of relative emphasis. In a literature course there should be some writing, which should be judged by the same standards that apply in a composition course. In a compositon course there should be some reading, which ought to include as much material of literary worth as possible.

To give adequate instruction in a sufficient range of literature and to acquaint the student with necessary principles of language, logic, and rhetoric while giving him enough practice in composition, a single year-long course obviously affords too little time. Many colleges and universities have recognized this fact and have prescribed a year of composition and a year of literature, in the belief that a firm grounding in both is necessary for the liberally educated adult. This is the pattern that other colleges ought to work toward. To ask for more than this might seem unreasonable, considering the demands of other fields of learning; to be content with less is to do a disservice to the study of English in college.

Meanwhile, many colleges must be content with less—with a single year of required English in which the claims of both literature and composition must be met. It is far from an ideal arrangement, but much can still be done even in this limited time. Half of such a year-long course ought to be given mainly to the study of literature, probably the second half; as much writing as possible should be assigned, but it should mainly serve the purposes of the instruction in literature. In the other half of the course, the reverse should hold true; the literature read should serve the ends of composition teaching and should consist mainly of good expository prose, which would be closely related to the kind of writing that students are being taught to master.

16. *Suggestions for a pattern of freshman English courses.* It would be rash to try to prescribe dogmatically a certain kind of

course or a particular pattern of courses in freshman English for all colleges. Colleges vary too much in size, in kind of students, in administrative structure, and in curricular organization for a single kind of course or sequence of courses to make equally good sense on every campus. Moreover, the teaching of composition is an art, not a science, and can be approached in many ways with apparently almost equal success. The suggestions ventured here, then, are put forward with proper cautiousness.

The general nature of such suggestions has been made clear in the earlier parts of this report. Briefly, a desirable pattern would consist of a year of literature for sophomores so as to leave room for a full year of composition for freshmen. A year course in composition ought to give approximately equal attention to logic, language, and rhetoric, probably in that order, with constant practice in writing extending through the year. Some of the writing would be exercises intended to clarify subject matter or enforce principles of logic or rhetoric; but most of it would be organized essays on a variety of subjects, usually related to assigned reading but focused whenever possible on a specific writing problem. Good expository prose would be studied; and, for an occasional change of pace, perhaps a little fiction might be included.

When only a single year of required English is provided, logic and rhetoric (and possibly some language study) should make up half the course, literature the other half. The writing in the composition half of the course would be like that just described; in the literature half, the writing would be analysis and criticism of the literary works being studied.

In providing a specific example, the second pattern will be assumed since it is much more common that the first. For the same reason, the two-semester plan will be assumed rather than the quarter system. In a fifteen-week semester devoted to a composition course of the kind suggested here, perhaps 20 per cent of the term could be given to the study of logic, another 20 per cent to language, 40 per cent to rhetoric (ordinarily through analysis and discussion of expository prose selections), and 20 per cent to class discussion of student writing. If classes are small, this last could be reduced to 10 per cent, and the teacher could discuss the writing of more students in conference; the other 10 per cent might then be given to prose fiction to vary the course from time to time or to provide a bridge at the end to the literature course that is to follow. If the staff is not qualified to give instruction in language of the sort recommended here, language study could be omitted, and the amount of time given to logic and rhetoric could be increased accordingly.

The work on logic ought to include a study of definition, evidence, induction, and deduction as they bear on expository composition. The rhetorical principles involved in writing good exposition ought to be derived, as far as possible, from a close analysis of expository selections and should include a consideration of purpose, focus (limiting a subject, adjusting it to purpose and reader), point of view, tone, structure, paragraphs, sentences, diction. This work would constitute, actually, a close study of expository prose style. The work on language, if included, would necessarily have to be even more selective than that on logic because of the great variety of topics that might be used. Choice need not be narrowly restricted to certain topics, so long as the particular topics chosen can be treated fully enough in the time available to whet the student's interest in language as a worthy subject of study and in some measure enlighten rather than muddle him. The sources of correctness in English might be one such topic; an introduction to linguistic geography—what it is, how it assembles its data, what its claims to interest are—might be another.

The writing assignments should be varied. Some ought to be frankly designated as exercises—an expanded definition perhaps, or the close analysis of a passage of prose to separate fact from opinion or inference, or a short composition consciously attempting to imitate or even parody the style of a given author. Some might be analyses of the style of selected essays—a discussion of tone and point of view in Orwell's "Shooting an Elephant," a study of sentence structure in Russell's "A Free Man's Worship," an analysis of the structure of an entire essay by Arnold or Hazlitt or E. M. Forster. Still others might be essays based on ideas found in the readings or criticisms of these ideas—a comparison of Newman's idea of the purpose of university education (in "What Is a University?") with the student's own notions of higher education; or, after reading Thoreau's "Civil Disobedience," an essay on peace marchers or freedom riders or some other kind of social protest with which students may be particularly familiar. The focus in this kind of assignment should be on the quality of the reasoning, the sufficiency of the evidence, and the effectiveness of the expression, not on the teacher's view of the worth of the opinions or the student's right to hold them. Toward the end of the course students might be given some practice in writing critical papers based on the study of imaginative literature—prose fiction—as a direct preparation for the following course.

The earlier work in analysis and composition should also help prepare students for the literature course; not only should they be able at the end of the first course to write more fluently, correctly, and cogently than when they began, but they should also have learned something about style and how to go about analyzing and evaluating it. Moreover, they should have gained a considerable acquaintance with distinguished examples of exposition, a kind of prose that they must read and write extensively in the years to come; and through this study they should have become somewhat more discriminating readers and writers of expository prose.

As for the literature course in the second half of the year, it could be organized in several ways, including the way in which Dartmouth's English 1 is now organized: several plays by Shakespeare and *Paradise Lost*, or some other selection of undoubted masterpieces chosen solely for their literary merit. Or the course could be organized by genre or by chronology or by some thematic element. Probably organization by genre is best for a required freshman course. By acquainting the student with a wide range of types, authors, and periods, it may do more to encourage wide and informed reading in after years than a course centered on a few masterpieces. A leading assumption behind the latter kind of course is that by becoming familiar with the works of several of the undoubted giants of English literature, the student will develop standards of taste founded on the best rather than the next-to-best. There is merit in the argument; but if works in a genre course are selected with due care, they can help the student form criteria of taste that are entirely adequate.

A genre course could include a play or two by Shakespeare, and perhaps part of *Paradise Lost* as well, but it should include other plays also and a judicious selection of narrative and lyric verse. Novels might comprise one unit of the course, even when a limited study of prose fiction has been made at the end of the first course. In the earlier course it might be wise to choose from among relatively short works written in this century and likely to have a strong immediate appeal—Conrad's *Heart of Darkness* or *Typhoon*, Hemingway's *A Farewell to Arms*, Fitzgerald's *The Great Gatsby*. The second course then might profitably require the close study of several of the unquestioned masterpieces of English and American fiction—*Vanity Fair, Tom Jones, Pride and Prejudice, Moby Dick*.

There should be as much writing in the second course as in the first. The papers ought usually to be analysis and criticism of the literature and should be short (700 to 800 words) more often than long. The reason is that students have a better chance to form habits of good writing if they have written repeatedly, each time confronting a different subject, collecting and ordering their ideas about it, putting them down in a complete composition. The preparation of the long research paper that so often is a part of the second-term freshman English course necessarily reduces the number of times that a student goes through the entire process of composing. Besides, there is really no reason why the English department more than any other department should feel responsible for introducing the student to the methods of doing research in secondary sources. All departments share in this task.

Teacher Preparation

17. *Suggestions for a curriculum to prepare teachers of English composition.* College English departments have often complained of the inadequate preparation of many of the English teachers in the schools. But college English departments have too seldom recognized the extent of their own culpability not only for inexpert teaching in the schools but for teaching in their own freshman English courses that often is even less expert and less informed. A principal reason for this situation is that both the undergraduate and the graduate curricula in English for the prospective teacher, whether school or college, have long consisted almost entirely of courses in literature, as though literature is all that English teachers are ever asked to teach; or, if they are asked to teach language and composition, as though a knowledge of literature mysteriously but surely carries with it the ability to teach language and composition.

This attitude reveals an almost perverse disregard by college English departments of the plain facts. Practically every college

English teacher must, for his first eight or ten years in the profession, spend a large part of his time teaching freshman composition. And if he is not prepared to teach it, he not only serves his students ill but he is often forced into a position that compromises his integrity as a professional person. That is, either he tries to teach what he is charged with teaching but does it poorly because he is not competent in it, or he pays scant attention to what he is supposed to teach and concentrates on what he really wants to teach because he is competent in it: literature. It reflects little credit on college English departments that so many of them for so long have tolerated this state of affairs—even, by their neglect, encouraged it. The time has come for them to accept the rest of their proper responsibilities.

The following suggestions for changes in the preparation of young people who plan to become college English teachers are based on the assumption that a course in composition will continue to be required for most students, probably in the freshman year, and that (hopefully) it will be a better course than many of those now being offered, one that is genuinely of college grade. A course of this sort, similar perhaps to the one proposed in Recommendation 16, would make the need for adequate teacher preparation even more urgent. Its greater rigor and sharper focus on subject matter directly relevant to composition would place demands on the teacher that few of the existing patterns of courses for prospective college English teachers take much account of.

A more realistic curriculum must be fashioned to prepare teachers to teach composition in college with the same expertness that they bring to the teaching of literature. Such a curriculum ought to have three specific aims: to make the teacher a good writer himself, to make him a good critic of writing, and to acquaint him with some of the practical problems that will confront him in the composition classroom and to suggest ways of dealing with them.

a. To ensure that the prospective teacher is able to write good prose, he shoud first be required to take a solid course in freshman composition. If as a freshman he was one of those rare students who have somehow already developed a firm and clear prose style, he could be exempted from the course; but he should not be allowed to skip it, as many prospective English majors now do, simply because he spells correctly and puts all his commas in the right places. Second, when he is a junior or senior, he should be asked to take an advanced course in composition, whether or not he has been exempted from the freshman course. This course should combine frequent writing assignments, of a mature kind, with a systematic study of rhetorical theory. Third, all the papers and examinations that the prospective teacher prepares for his English courses, both undergraduate and graduate, should be carefully read with an eye to the quality of the prose as well as to the accuracy and cogency of the statements; and the grade should reflect this scrutiny. Finally, his master's thesis and doctoral dissertation should be closely supervised by his advisor or his committee to make sure that they are written in correct, lucid, and vigorous English. It is no secret that at present, few English majors who go on to advanced degrees enjoy the last two of these advantages.

b. The literature courses already in the English curriculum, both undergraduate and graduate, should go far toward helping the future teacher become a sound critic of writing, provided these courses are taught with a recognition that this is one of their proper objectives. That is, the literature courses ought, among other things, to give the future English teacher practice in analysis and evaluation, should encourage him to deduce important rhetorical principles from the literature studied, and should help him to develop a sure sense of literary quality.

Courses in language can also contribute. At a minimum the required work in language should include a course in the history of English and another in the structure of modern English. Together they ought to give the future teacher an informed point of view toward present-day English in the light of its historical development, should furnish him with a detailed knowledge of the structure of English sentences, and should enable him to develop a reasoned attitude toward matters of usage.

As a further means of developing critical ability, an undergraduate course in logic ought to be required of all prospective teachers of English. And a final requirement should be a graduate course in English prose style, so organized as to include both a historical survey and intensive practice in analysis. The kind of information and training provided by such a course is important for the teacher of composition, especially when he teaches at the college level, yet it is seldom available now except piecemeal.

c. As for introducing the prospective teacher to the problems of the composition classroom—making assignments, marking and grading papers, leading class discussions, and the like—English departments should take fuller advantage of the fact that most of their doctoral candidates and many of their candidates for master's degrees are or could be engaged in part-time teaching of freshman composition. But two extremes of current practice should be avoided. On the one hand, it would be a mistake to follow the lead of some universities at which the young teacher, having been given a handbook, a book of readings, a syllabus, and the number of the room where he is to teach, is turned loose on a class as inexperienced with college study as he is with college teaching. Nor is the opposite plan any better: unloading on the prospective teacher such menial jobs as taking roll in someone else's course and correcting routine quizzes but never letting him take full charge of a class. A middle ground is best, an intelligently supervised apprenticeship that allows the beginning teacher both to observe the skillful teaching of an experienced colleague to whom he is assigned and to teach under gradually reduced supervision. It need hardly be added that the success of such an arrangement depends largely on whether the senior member of the partnership is indeed a good teacher and whether he is blessed with a large measure of tact.

A program of in-service training such as this will give the beginning teacher actual classroom experience, while at the same time helping him to correct some mistakes and avoid others. It should also instill in him a sense of responsibility toward the profession he has chosen. Such programs, thoroughly planned and conscientiously supervised, already exist at some universities—not, unfortunately, at all.

RECOMMENDATIONS FOR WRITING AFTER THE FRESHMAN YEAR

The recommendations below are based on several conclusions to which the discussion of writing proficiency at Dartmouth and elsewhere has pointed: (1) The great majority of students who pass freshman English with grades of C or above at reputable four-year colleges and universities can write reasonably well or better when they know they must, but often they are reprehensibly slipshod. (2) A steady pressure to write well must be exerted on college students throughout their undergraduate years; the more opportunities that can be provided for them to write careful prose, the better their chances of developing a decent prose style. (3) College students are too seldom asked by their other teachers to do as much careful writing as they should. Many conscientious teachers who would be willing to assign more writing and to read it carefully are unable to do so because of the large size of their classes; others frankly admit their inability to judge prose expertly for quality except in the most superficial aspects; still others are convinced, sincerely if mistakenly, that they have no responsibility in the matter and that good student writing is the business of the English department. (4) Any writing that students do in a college course should be judged for its quality as English prose as well as for considerations that rise more directly from the demands of the subject itself. (5) Poor writing should be penalized just as poor thinking is penalized; in most subjects the two are indistinguishable.

18. *A check on students with low grades in freshman English.* Most students who earn a pair of D's or a D and a low C in freshman English do not have a secure grasp on the technique of good writing and should be watched closely during their remaining three years. Some provision should be made for remanding the weakest of these students for further instruction of some sort if their performance after they have completed freshman English shows that they are still writing at, say, a D level. Moral suasion might do the job for some: let it be known that two D's or a D and a low C in freshman English confer only provisional credit, which will not be validated until late in the senior year and then only if the student's writing has been satisfactory in all the courses he has taken. Other such students may need more instruction. Private tutoring would be the best solution, for to send them back to repeat a freshman English course would be to work a hardship on more people than just these students themselves.

19. *A statement of policy on writing.* A college or university faculty should endorse an official statement of policy on student writing. The statement ought to include at least four main points: (*a*) The college or university recognizes that a clear, correct, and responsible use of language is a principal hallmark of an educated man. (*b*) The faculty has therefore agreed that grades on papers

that are ill-written, no matter what the course, may be reduced for the quality of the writing alone. (*c*) The faculty has also agreed that course grades may be lowered for persistently careless or otherwise substandard writing; in extreme cases a failing grade may be given for this reason alone. (*d*) The college or university cannot afford to confer a degree on a student whose careless and imprecise use of language betrays a careless and imprecise intelligence; good writing is therefore a prerequisite to graduation.

Such a statement will inevitably be taken seriously by some students and faculty members and ignored by others. But if the faculty, as a community of scholars and teachers, has the regard that it should for the integrity of language and a sense of the responsibility one incurs in using language, a statement of principle should be formulated to make clear where the faculty stands and what the avowed attitude of the institution itself is toward the use of language by the students who are being educated there. And when any teacher chooses to insist on a higher quality of writing from his students, he will have the official backing of his colleagues when he does so.

20. *A "Committee on Student English."* An institution-wide Committee on Student English, when strongly supported by the college or university administration and vigorously led by an able chairman, can have a salutary effect on the general quality of student writing after the freshman year even if it cannot hope to solve the problem of poor writing in any final sense. Such a committee ought therefore to be appointed at any college or university that is seriously concerned to raise the level of student writing in all courses and keep it as high as possible. The committee ought usually to be fairly large—ten or twelve members—and, so as to command the widest support among the faculty, ought to include equal representation from the various divisions of the institution, with no department (including English) contributing more than one member. It is especially important that the committee not be dominated, in appearance or in fact, by the English department, which may be thought to be whetting a private ax or cultivating a private garden plot whenever the committee makes a recommendation. College or university administrative officers, who quite properly have a direct interest in the work of the committee, should serve on it only ex officio; the committee should be entirely a *faculty* agency,

immune to any possible charge of administrative influence. It would be better if the chairman of the committee were to come from some department other than English. Whatever success the committee may enjoy will depend largely on the degree to which the committee is, and is recognized to be, an institution-wide group serving the interests of the institution as a whole.

The principal business of the committee should be to attempt to make the question of student writing an issue on the campus. It should endeavor to awaken the faculty to the importance of good writing in a scheme of liberal education and to persuade as many teachers as possible to require as much writing as the nature of the particular subject allows and to judge it by standards appropriate to an institution of higher learning. There is unfortunately no formula to show how these aims can be accomplished, but some of the devices being used at various colleges might be put to the test elsewhere. For example, if the English department of a college follows an earlier recommendation of this report and draws up a specific list of gross errors in composition, the committee might find it profitable to endorse the list for general use and distribute it to the entire faculty with a recommendation that such errors be looked for in student papers and severely penalized. The committee might explore the possibility of securing a copy of a good handbook of English grammar and usage for every member of the teaching faculty; such a book ought at least in theory to encourage some teachers to mark papers more thoroughly for the quality of writing; and, if it is the right book, a certain amount of adult education might take place.[5]

The committee might also try to discover and publicize any devices that other members of the faculty have developed to secure better writing from their students. The questionnaire sent to the Dartmouth faculty turned up two that will serve as examples. A teacher of an advanced mathematics course assigns students in turn to write up detailed class notes which he then duplicates and

[5] It might, for example, make a dent in several superstitions about language: that correct writing and good writing are synonymous; that correctness in language is an either-or matter; that books of grammar and dictionaries lay down laws; and so on. The most damaging criticism that can be made of past instruction in English grammar and usage in school and college is the almost universal misunderstanding of the nature of these subjects that one finds among even the most highly educated people today.

distributes to the other members of the class. He reports that students take pride in preparing a lucid and well-organized set of notes for their classmates, who are a critical audience. Several teachers of advanced courses in science assign students to write papers in the form of essays to be submitted to professional journals in the particular field; the assignment has the advantage of specifying form, audience, tone, and point of view—and there is always the off-chance of actual publication to stimulate good performance.

Such a committee should not expect, nor should it be expected, to perform a miracle and turn all teachers into accomplished critics with a passion for good prose and all students into embryonic professional writers gifted with unfailing fluency, disciplined thought, and a discriminating sense of style. What it may hope to accomplish will be very modest and often hard to detect in tangible ways. But the effort is worth making even for modest gains.

21. *Disciplined practice in writing in courses other than freshman English.* As this report has frequently pointed out, all the evidence suggests that the best—perhaps the only—way to keep students writing as well as possible after they have finished their freshman English course is to maintain a steady pressure on them to do so. One may quite properly feel that college students should be mature enough intellectually to recognize the value of writing well on all occasions and to do so habitually, without threat or inducement; but it is evident that few of them do. Some need the carrot, others the stick. Most of the devices that have been tried in an effort to exert this pressure on students have failed. At best, they have worked for only a year or two while the novelty lasted, then have fallen into disuse. Writing clinics to which poor writers may be referred, proficiency examinations, conditions on grades, threats to withhold degrees—none of these is entirely without value, but none has been very successful.

Ideally, the pressure to write well could best be exerted if every teacher of a class in which the writing of connected prose is appropriate would assign as much writing as he could, read and mark it as carefully as an English teacher would, and take the quality of the writing into account when assigning grades. But, for reasons mentioned earlier, such a happy state of affairs is not likely to come about. A reasonable compromise would be to seek some way of ensuring that each student in at least one course every year is expected to write often and well. If a college has any institution-wide programs like Dartmouth's General Reading Program or Great Issues course, it has a perfect opportunity to exert in particular years the kind of pressure needed, provided it takes steps to avoid the difficulties that have attended the writing practice in the Dartmouth programs. These troubles could be largely eliminated by making sure that such programs confer an amount of course credit appropriate to the amount of work required of the students and that the writing is competently read and criticized, preferably by people especially hired for the purpose and given special training to qualify them for the job.

Colleges that do not have such programs ought then to do the next best thing: identify several large courses in the sophomore, junior, and senior years in which it would be appropriate to assign more writing and which, taken together, enroll the great majority of students each year. A number of readers should then be found in the community who are competent in the subject of the course; they should be trained in evaluation of prose composition and assigned to read and grade the additional written work. Such an arrangement would be much less expensive than a general reduction in class size and much more feasible than an effort to train teachers of physics or anthropology or political science to read papers as an English teacher would. Even if the size of classes were reduced to a point where the teachers who say they would like to assign more writing could actually do so without unduly burdening themselves, it is by no means certain that they would all assign more writing. More than a few would surely spend this windfall of extra time, if it materialized, on research in their field of specialization, an understandable and by no means blameworthy option.

In a college community it should not be hard to find enough college-educated women who majored in the right subjects when they were undergraduates. More often than not, however, they will have only an intelligent layman's competence in grammar, rhetoric, and usage. At the beginning of each year a series of meetings for the readers should be planned at which someone from the English department could work with then on marking and evaluating typical papers, acquaint them with accepted standards of usage, point out and explain rhetorical problems, and give them an informed attitude toward English grammar. And just as it is desirable for an English staff to meet periodically throughout the year for paper-grading sessions so that standards can be kept in line, so would it be equally valuable for the readers to meet several times a year for this purpose. The better the readers are able to criticize and grade the papers, the more valuable the experience of writing the papers will be for the students.

Appendixes

APPENDIX A

Exempting Students from Freshman English

The notion of excusing entering freshmen from college requirements that they have already fulfilled, either through independent study or through course work in the lower schools, is not new. For many years most colleges have had among their regulations a provision to give credit for a course by special examination. And the practice is well established of giving placement tests in mathematics and foreign languages to determine the level of course that a student should be enrolled in. Placement tests in English have also been given for at least a generation, and on the basis of test results a few freshmen often have been exempted from all or part of the usual requirement in freshman English. More commonly, high-scoring students have been placed in special "high" sections of the freshman course that supposedly are designed with their needs in view.

In the last half dozen years the demand for greater educational rigor to meet the challenge of Russian scientific success has encouraged efforts not only to improve the education of superior students but to speed it up. As a consequence, pressure has mounted sharply to exempt able students from elementary college courses whenever they can furnish evidence that they have already gained equivalent skill or knowledge. The Advanced Placement Program, which has established college-level courses in many high schools, has been an increasingly powerful influence in this direction. Even more influential has been the movement for curriculum reform in high school mathematics, foreign language, and science, as a result of which more and more of the responsibility of giving elementary instruction in these subjects is being transferred from the colleges to the high schools.

Freshman English is perhaps the likeliest of all the courses in the freshman year from which able students might seek to be exempted.

Far too often it has been a thinly disguised high school course, repeating once more the familiar "review of fundamentals" and the theme assignments on favorite teachers and happy vacations. But in spite of pressure from Advanced Placement courses in English and the trend toward accelerating the education of bright students, there is still no sign among college English departments of a general agreement on what to do about exempting students from the freshman course. At one extreme, Harvard College, which has perhaps the most select freshman class in the country, exempts no one from the requirement in "General Education A" ("English Composition") except students who have transferred to Harvard with credit for a comparable course at another college, and students who present a grade of 4 or 5 on the Advanced Placement test in English *and* have enough Advanced Placement credits in other courses as well to qualify at once for sophomore standing. At the other extreme, Princeton makes no pretense of offering a course in English composition. Instead, freshmen may elect one of several literature courses; in each of the two most frequently taken, three 1,200-word papers are written.

Most other colleges fall somewhere between these extremes, but confusion is the norm. A privately controlled university in the Midwest, which had a freshman class in 1961–1962 of about six hundred (mean score on SAT Verbal: 657), gives total exemption to the top 11 per cent and exempts another 30 per cent from one term of the three-term sequence. Another privately controlled university, this one in the Southeast, with a freshman class of about eleven hundred (mean score on SAT Verbal: 588), exempts no one but Advanced Placement students who have grades of three, four, or five—in 1961–1962, twenty-one students. Another university in the Ivy League exempts 15 per cent from the first-semester course, and excuses all those who get A or B in the first course (22 per cent) from the second. Still another in the Ivy League exempts 5 per cent from the first-semester course, as does a publicly supported university on the West Coast. A Big Ten university, which must accept all graduates from accredited high schools in the state, in 1961–1962 exempted almost 50 per cent of the freshman class from one semester of the freshman requirement and put them in a special one-semester accelerated course; 4 or 5 per cent were granted total exemption. A sister university in the same state, drawing students from the same high schools and bound by the same admission regulations, in the same year exempted 4 per cent from one term of a three-term sequence and put another 26 per cent in "high" sections that run the full year. And so on.

There are several explanations to account for this chaos. One is that curriculum reforms of the sort that have been so effective in raising the level of instruction in foreign languages, science, and mathematics in the high schools are just getting started in English. The next five years should see considerable progress in rationalizing the high school curriculum in English, with important consequences for freshman English in college. Another explanation is that there is no easily defined body of knowledge in the subject we call English that is clearly antecedent to a college course in English. In mathematics, science, and foreign languages, the curriculum is sequential and cumulative in a way that is not possible in English. It is an advantage for a student to have read the Bible before reading Milton, and classical mythology before reading Spenser or Keats, but it is not prerequisite in the way that algebra is to trigonometry or first-year French to second-year French. For this reason it is difficult to say with certainty what work ought to be assigned to the schools and what to the colleges. The closest approach to such a division is to say that entering freshmen ought to have learned in high school to write reasonably well; and if they have, they should be exempted from freshman English. The trouble is that it is difficult to agree on what "reasonably well" means, with the result that some colleges are hard to satisfy, some easy, and exemption policy varies accordingly.

Most important of all, the attitude toward exemption from freshman English depends largely on the convictions that a particular English department holds about the freshman course and on the particular course that has grown out of those convictions. Specifically, the question is whether a department regards freshman English as a "service" course, which exists to equip the student with a minimum competence in reading and writing so that he will not founder in his other courses; or whether a department looks on this course as one that has a humane function: to discipline the student's thinking and his powers of expression, as a means not merely of helping him pass his other courses but of making him more interesting and successful as a human being. A department that holds the former view is likely to favor a generous exemption policy; one that holds the latter will probably resist exempting students from the freshman course, or will want to exempt relatively few.

It is difficult to view the question of exemption clearly, because a reasonable attitude toward it must take account of a great many circumstances that will vary widely from one institution to the next—caliber of students, quality of their preparation in English, type of freshman English course, the philosophy underlying it, qualifications of the freshman English staff, and so on. But one can take a step toward a clearer view by examining the arguments on both sides of the question.

Against exempting students from freshman English it can be argued that writing is a skill that is infinitely perfectible and that it is folly to be satisfied with a minimum level of accomplishment when so much more is possible. With the quality of student now being admitted to most four-year colleges and universities steadily rising from year to year, a good instructor assigned to a good course should be able to teach writing in a real sense, not merely labor to eliminate errors in grammar and usage. If the course is one that is based on language, rhetoric, or logic, it can be argued that these are all humane disciplines worthy of serious study in college and that students cannot already have learned everything about them that a liberally educated adult ought to know. If the course is based on literature, this again is a humane study worthy for its own sake as well as for its bearing on the teaching of composition. In short, instead of exempting the best students from freshman English, one may argue that a new course should be offered for them which would deal with humane studies at a more advanced level and that would endeavor to raise skill in writing from competence to distinction. Finally, the fact is that even at the most select colleges not many freshmen write so well at entrance that they could not profit from a rigorous course in composition. Few of them, it is true, have serious trouble with the mechanics of writing; but the great majority would benefit from further instruction in the rhetoric and logic of expository prose.

On the other side, it should first be pointed out that it is easy enough to say writing is a skill that has no top limit and that a student who enters college already able to write A papers can and should be taught to write even better. But it is considerably more difficult to set up a course in which this kind of instruction can be given; and it is more difficult still to find teachers who can successfully give it. Many colleges have established honor sections of their freshman course in which superior students are enrolled. In these courses there is usually more reading, and more difficult reading; writing assignments are nearly always longer and there may be more of them; but very rarely is anything done to teach writing on a more advanced level—to teach advanced rhetoric, for example, or those aspects of logic that pertain most directly to the writing of analysis and criticism. The courses are most commonly ones in literature, sometimes with more writing required than in the usual literature course, sometimes not. The difficulty seems to be that few English teachers know enough about the teaching of writing (especially the "non-creative" kinds) at these higher levels. Or perhaps the trouble is that writing cannot be taught at this level in a classroom situation but must be managed in individual conferences, a methed prohibitively expensive.

Another point favoring exemption is that there is nothing sacred about *four* years of college. If a student who has unusual ability and unusual energy is able to get a sound education in less than four years by being exempted from courses whose content he has already mastered, he should be allowed—even encouraged—to do so. It is important to remember that not all learning must be done in numbered courses meeting three times a week. Another argument for exemption, related to the one just mentioned, is that the conditions of modern society make it highly desirable to shorten the time of a student's preparation to assume adult responsibilities, especially if he plans to enter one of the professions. Partly because of the pattern of population increase, all the professions are seriously understaffed and will be for some years to come. But whether he enters a profession or not, a student is forced by the cost of college study in both dollars and time to take advantage of all short cuts that do not compromise the quality of his education. Finally, as far as freshman English is concerned, it is obvious that some students come to college who, no matter how or where they have learned, are able to think and write well enough to do excellent work at once. With considerable labor and ingenuity, a course in composition could be set up for them that, if well taught, would meet them where they are and advance them further. But one must ask at this point whether the value of such a course would be greater for them than that of some other course they need or want to take or greater than the gain in time saved if they choose not to take another course in place of the one they are excused from. To allow no exemption at all is a counsel of perfection.

These arguments on both sides of the question are all defensible and legitimate. But other arguments of more dubious validity seem often to be affecting the policy toward exemption on many campuses. On the one hand, a protective attitude by some English departments (or groups within the departments) toward the freshman course sometimes serves to discourage exemption. It is freshman English that makes the English department always the largest in a college or university, both in class enrollments and in faculty. Not surprisingly, those who rule the considerable empires that sometimes develop may be reluctant to see their domains reduced by large-scale exemptions from freshman English. And in universities where large numbers of graduate students are employed to teach freshman English, graduate professors may argue wryly, but with some justice, that making substantial reductions in freshman English enrollments will cut down the number of part-time teaching jobs for graduate students in English. And unless such opportunities are available, the supply of qualified English teachers, already declining at an alarming rate, will become hopelessly inadequate to meet the greatly increased college enrollments expected in the near future.

On the other hand, arguments for a more generous policy on exemption are heard from two sources. First are those English professors who disdain the freshman course—indeed, sometimes disdain all undergraduate instruction—and would be pleased to see not simply more exemptions from the course but its abolition. In fairness to this point of view, it must be said that there is truth in the charge that a great many freshman English courses as now constituted are not of college caliber. Their textbooks are not of the same order of intellectual rigor as those for beginning courses in other subjects; the activity that goes in the courses often differs little, if at all, in either kind or difficulty, from that in eleventh or twelfth grade English; and the teachers assigned to freshman English are often less well prepared by their undergraduate and graduate study to teach the course than are high school teachers to teach those courses assigned them. The weakness of this view is that it is over-hasty and undiscriminating. Not all freshman English courses are blots on the college curriculum; some are sound, rigorous courses, and their merits should be taken into account when assessing freshman English in general and its probable future.

The other source of arguments for a higher rate of exemption is college and university administrative officers, who, in this day of competition among colleges for bright students, are alert to discover "selling points" whenever possible. If College Y and University Z, which compete directly with College X for students, are reported to be exempting a quarter of all freshmen from freshman English, voices may soon be raised at College X suggesting that a third—perhaps a half?—of all freshmen enrolling at College X be promised exemption from freshman English. This action will put College X's recruiters in a strong position to attract good students away from the competing schools.

It is over this last aspect of the exemption problem that classroom teachers and college or university administrative officials are most likely to disagree. Neither group can see much reasonableness in the view of the other. Teachers, insulated from the strenuous competition that now goes on for bright students, are likely to oversimplify the admissions officers' problems and to undervalue the importance of such inducements to enrollment as the promise of exemption from basic courses or special privileges in choosing a course of study in the freshman year. Now that brains and intellectual distinction are at last becoming fashionable in American colleges, some teachers will allege that admissions officials have begun recruiting bright students much as, a few years ago, they recruited promising halfbacks or well-rounded future organization men. They may hint that in their opinion institutional prestige is the goal of this recruiting more than educational excellence and that the same sort of vicarious satisfaction is now being derived from association with a college whose freshmen average 650 on the SAT Verbal test as used to be gained from being connected with a college that had a winning football team.

Above all, teachers are likely to be unhappy about what they regard as the perverse way in which a course they work hard at may be used as enrollment bait: The bright student is urged to enroll at the college not so that he will have the opportunity to take this course but so that he will enjoy the privilege of not having to take it. The notion is not calculated to flatter either course or teacher.

Admissions officials, on the other hand, cannot understand why teachers should cavil over admissions policies and procedures if the result of these policies and procedures is to place better students in the teachers' classrooms. They may freely admit that institutional prestige is one of the goals of their activities: If prestige declines, so do donations, grants, and other income. But they will also insist with some spirit that their principal aim is to give the teachers in their institution the best available raw material from which the teachers are to fashion educated adults. The better the student, the more the teacher should be able to do for him, and the more the student should later contribute to adult society. If the intellectual quality of students admitted to the institution began to decline noticeably, admissions officials are confident that they would hear promptly and emphatically from the teachers. They therefore regard the attitude of many teachers toward exemption as wrong-headed, unrealistic, and contradictory.

Perhaps it would be fair to sum up the whole matter by saying (what indeed is obvious) that the ruling consideration in exemption policy ought always to be the intellectual welfare of the particular student, as far as this can be determined. A freshman course in composition, if it is to deserve a place in a college curriculum, must first of all be genuinely of college level. If it is, it will not simply traverse again the ground covered in high school English but will perceptibly advance the student's intellectual development. From such a course some students will still deserve to be exempted, but wholesale exemptions will be hard to justify. Institutional prestige, competition for able freshmen, or a desire to provide employment for graduate students may all bear on exemption policy in some degree, but they obviously should not be allowed to determine it.

APPENDIX B

A Suggested Minimum Bibliography for Composition Teachers

RHETORIC

Plato. *Georgias* and *Phaedrus*.

Aristotle. *Rhetoric*.

Cooper, Lane, ed. *Theories of Style, with Especial Reference to Prose Composition*. New York: The Macmillan Company, 1907.

Graves, Robert, and Alan Hodge. *The Reader over Your Shoulder: A Handbook for Writers of English Prose*. New York: The Macmillan Company, 1943.

Dobrée, Bonamy. *Modern Prose Style*. Oxford: The Clarendon Press, 1934.

Read, Herbert. *English Prose Style*. Boston: Beacon Press, 1952.

Boulton, Marjorie. *The Anatomy of Prose*. London: Routledge & Kegan Paul, Ltd., 1954.

None of the last three books mentioned above is very satisfactory, but these are so far the only books available that deal at all extensively with the style of factual (as opposed to imaginative) prose in general.

LOGIC

An introductory college-level logic text, such as:

Beardsley, M. C. *Practical Logic*. Englewood Cliffs, N.J.: Prentice-Hall, Inc., 1950.

Brennan, Joseph G. *A Handbook of Logic*, 2d ed. New York: Harper & Row, Publishers, 1957, 1961.

Copi, Irving M. *Introduction to Logic*. New York: The Macmillan Company, 1953.

LANGUAGE

A history of English, such as:

Baugh, Albert C. *A History of the English Language*, 2d ed. New York: Appleton-Century-Crofts, Inc., 1957.

Bryant, Margaret M. *Modern English and Its Heritage*, 2d ed. New York: The Macmillan Company, 1948, 1962.

Jespersen, Otto. *Growth and Structure of the English Language*. Garden City, N.Y.: Doubleday and Company, Inc., Anchor Book, 1955.

Robertson, Stuart. *The Development of Modern English*, rev. F. G. Cassidy. Englewood Cliffs, N.J.: Prentice-Hall, Inc., 1934, 1938, 1954.

A book on traditional grammar, such as:

Jespersen, Otto. *Essentials of English Grammar.* New York: Holt, Rinehart and Winston, Inc., 1933.

Roberts, Paul. *Understanding Grammar.* New York: Harper & Row, Publishers, 1954.

A book on language, such as:

Bloomfield, Leonard. *Language.* New York: Holt, Rinehart and Winston, Inc., 1933.

Sapir, Edward. *Language: An Introduction to the Study of Speech.* New York: Harcourt, Brace & World, Inc., Harvest Book, 1921, 1949.

Sturtevant, E. H. *An Introduction to Linguistic Science.* New Haven: Yale University Press, 1947.

A book on American English, such as:

Krapp, G. P. *The English Language in America,* 2 vols. New York: Appleton-Century-Crofts, Inc., 1925.

Marckwardt, Albert H. *American English.* New York: Oxford University Press, 1958.

Mencken, H. L. *The American Language,* 4th ed., rev. New York: Alfred A. Knopf, Inc., 1936.

An introductory book on structural linguistics, such as:

Francis, W. Nelson. *The Structure of American English.* New York: The Ronald Press Company, 1958.

Sledd, James. *A Short Introduction to English Grammar.* Chicago: Scott, Foresman and Company, 1959.

Whitehall, Harold. *Structural Essentials of English.* New York: Harcourt, Brace & World, Inc., 1951, 1956.

A reference book on English usage, such as:

Evans, Bergen, and Cornelia Evans. *A Dictionary of Contemporary American Usage.* New York: Random House, Inc., 1957.

Fowler, H. W. *A Dictionary of Modern English Usage.* Oxford: The Clarendon Press, 1926.

APPENDIX C

Two Failing Themes

Below are two themes that were failed by the teachers who received them. The first is from an English 1 class at Dartmouth and is a fair representative of the poorest writing that a Dartmouth English teacher is likely to get in this course. The second paper was received in a remedial English course at a state university. Not all papers received in remedial courses are so hopeless; but it is sobering for teachers at more selective institutions to reflect that at many other colleges and universities English classes may be populated by students capable of perpetrating such work, and the English staff is charged with the responsibility of moving these young people from their present state to a reasonable degree of literacy.

Shakespeare verses Olivier

The true mastery of Shakespeare was brought to full effect in Sir Laurence Olivier's production of Richard the Third. Olivier brought Shakespeare to the modern audience. An audience which did not understand the complete background of English battle for the throne, the imagination of the Elizabethan man, nor the customs and traditions of sixteenth century England. To make Richard III more understandable to the common man, Sir Laurence has scrambled scenes, added or left out parts from the original. With these adjustments he does not destroy the meaning, but he rather clarifies and accentuates the incidents. You are very much aware of Sir Laurence's tremendous ability as an actor. Without this quality all of his revisions would be lost.

To quote Olivier, "I want to make Richard a dangerous creature, not just a hog. He was a clever and admusing man as well as a villian." I believe he more than achieved his goal. The simple yet decisive inflections by Olivier in his voice and action made the play increasingly penetrating. It takes a master actor to produce these inflections. He must understand the playwrite, as well as the character. It was obvious understood both very well.

His knowledge of Shakespeare and his experience with the modern audience gave him the qualities to produce the masterpiece that we viewed. The alterations must have had wisdom behind them for as Sir Laurence states, "The reaction of the critics to my changes was astonishingly lenient." These changes are numerous, but almost all helped my understanding and enjoyment of the play.

Since there are many changes I will only give those which interested me most. Certainally the two coronation scenes added tremendous to the play as well as giving us a better understanding of the past happenings in the battle for the crown. His addition of Jane Shore was as well as being helpful in placing her in time it was definitely admusing. It also produced the sexual effect that Shakespeare meant by the "lavcivious pleasing of a flute." Another admusing and perfectly placed addition was that of the two little, old monks. They were in perfect parallel with Shakespeare's use of humor on tense moments. One particularly revealing and tense moment was when Richard had "given-in" to the demands that he become king and comes snaking down the bell rope anxious to have the first man to knell before him. Besides inserting lines and scenes Sir Laurence made other alterations.

A particularly significant change of Olivier's was the death of Richard. Here you saw Richard writhing in pain after being stabbed by a multitude of common soldiers. This incident is significant for two reasons. First the common man shows his feeling for Richard, a feeling of hatred. Second, the writhing indicates that is physically paying for the agony he has caused others. Another very outstanding change in Oliviers Richard III was the spliting of the wooing scene of Lady Anne into two parts. Personally I liked his version better. It seemed to be more sensible, for nobody is going to be as quickly overcome as Anne was in Shakespeare's version. As Sir Laurence staged it you felt she had time to think over Richard's advancement and was better prepared for Richard's second attempt.

To cut Shakespeare is said to be a very dangerous thing to do, but of all the cuts made by Olivier only one met with my personal disapproval. One of the incidents which I was very happy to see removed was the part of old Margaret. She was only a middleman between the Lanchaster and Yorkish influences. She also personifies the evil in the play. I believe that she confuses the already confusing tracing of families, and there is also no reason why more evil is needed, the play is full of it. The single part which I sorely missed was the murderers discussion before the death of Clarence. I was very curious of how the scene would be played, and how the second murderer would act his part. Needless to say I was disappointed to find it missing. My disappointment is not the only thing that bothered me. I just do not understand why Olivier cut a part that was definitely a Shakespearan trait. That being the divergent factor preceding a particularly horrible scene. I do not see the reason for this action and really do not think it was necessary.

Except for this incident I believe Sir Laurence Olivier's production of Richard the Third was truly excellent. The combination of unparalleled acting, superb screnining, and accurate revisions made it the best Shakespearean play I have ever seen. Its world wide acclaim certainly proves its excellence and appeal to the modern audience.

What I Expect to Get Out of Collage

I hoping to become a coach some day in the future. Becaus i always wants to teach kids how to play football and make good enough that they handle themself when they grow up and make them better citizen and have them to be better physical shape and I am going to tries, to make them learn, how to work together as team would do when their, out their on that football feild and in the class room to.

That is the reason I cam to college to learn how to become a football coach and teach a little be along with it. I am hoping to learn everything to do with physical edecation.

I always wants to be a coach back in junior high school.

I play football back in Junior high school and letter in it.

And play in high school team I where been unbeat in two years in row in Junior high. and we won championship three in row and took the State title in my first year in high school in my second year we took sixth in state and last we took scond.

Index